Elite • 214

World War II Infantry Fire Support Tactics

GORDON L. ROTTMAN

ILLUSTRATED BY PETER DENNIS
Series editor Martin Windrow

First published in Great Britain in 2016 by Osprey Publishing
PO Box 883, Oxford, OX1 9PL, UK
1385 Broadway, 5th Floor, New York, NY 10018, USA
E-mail: info@ospreypublishing.com

Osprey Publishing, part of Bloomsbury Publishing Plc

A CIP catalog record for this book is available from the British Library

Print ISBN: 978 1 4728 1546 0
PDF ebook ISBN: 978 1 4728 1547 7
ePub ISBN: 978 1 4728 1548 4

Editor: Martin Windrow
Index by Mark Swift
Typeset in Sabon and Myraid Pro
Originated by PDQ Media, Bungay, UK
Printed in China through Worldprint Ltd

16 17 18 19 20 10 9 8 7 6 5 4 3 2 1

Osprey Publishing supports the Woodland Trust, the UK's leading woodland conservation charity. Between 2014 and 2018 our donations will be spent on their Centenary Woods project in the UK.

www.ospreypublishing.com

AUTHOR'S NOTE AND ACKNOWLEDGMENTS

In this text, for brevity, we use the *postwar* term "Commonwealth" for non-British forces of wartime dominions and colonies then fighting for the British Crown – i.e. Canadian, Australian, New Zealand, Indian, and African.

The author is indebted to Tom Laemlein of Armor Plate Press, and to Nik Cornish at www.stavka,org.uk, for the use of photographs.

ARTIST'S NOTE

Readers may care to note that the original paintings from which the color plates in this book were prepared are available for private sale. All reproduction copyright whatsoever is retained by the Publishers. All inquiries should be addressed to:

Peter Dennis, "Fieldhead," The Park, Mansfield, Nottinghamshire NG18 2AT, UK

The Publishers regret that they can enter into no correspondence upon this matter

---

Abbreviations used in this text

AA	antiaircraft
AFV	armored fighting vehicle (tanks, tank destroyers, assault guns, halftracks, armored cars, scout cars, etc.)
AP	armor-piercing
AT	antitank
BAR	M1918A2 Browning automatic rifle (pronounced "B-A-R")
Bde	brigade (British – formation of three infantry battalions)
CP	command post
cwt	hundredweight (112lb, one-twentieth of an Imperial ton – British weight measurement)
FO/FOO	forward observer/forward observation officer
HE	high explosive
HEAT	high-explosive antitank (shaped-charge projectile – pronounced "heat")

HMG	heavy machine gun
HQ	headquarters
LMG	light machine gun
MG	machine gun
MLR	main line of resistance (the frontline)
MMG	medium machine gun
Mtn	mountain
NCO	non-commissioned officer (corporal, sergeant)
OP	observation post
pdr	pounder (British gun caliber designation – see below)
PIAT	projector, infantry, antitank (British; pronounced "pee-at")
rpm	rounds per minute
SP	self-propelled
WP	white phosphorus (incendiary smoke-round filling)

Weapon calibers:

Most British AT guns and artillery pieces were designated by the rounded-off weight of the standard projectile, e.g. "25-pounder" (25-pdr). In first use in this text the caliber is also given in inches and/or millimeters.

German weapons smaller than 15mm (.59cal) were designated in millimeters. Those of larger caliber were designated in centimeters (e.g. 7.5cm = 75mm). Soviet weapons used a different millimeter scale.

Contemporary US customary linear measurements (in, ft, yd) and weights (oz, lb) are used here rather than metric.

CONTENTS

WORLD WAR II INFANTRY FIRE SUPPORT TACTICS

INTRODUCTION

The German version of the ubiquitous Brandt medium-caliber mortar was the 8cm mGrW 34. This was at first designated the sGrW 34, being rated as a heavy (*schwere*) mortar, but with the adoption of the 12cm sGrW 42 from 1942 the 8cm was redesignated as medium (*mittlerer*) class. In the foreground is an airtight steel ammunition case for three rounds. (Tom Laemlein/Armor Plate Press)

The term "fire support" covers a broad range of weapons, dedicated specialist units, tactics, and capabilities. Fire support includes weapons found at all echelons of units: machine guns, mortars, infantry guns, and AT guns and rifles. This book focuses on infantry fire support tactics and weapons at company, battalion, and regimental/brigade levels.

These weapons were essential in both the attack and defense, providing responsive fires; owing to the complexity of warfare and constantly changing doctrine and tactics, they were also frequently employed in manners not originally envisaged. Warfare changed so quickly at the tactical level that units more often developed their own employment techniques. Often there was no single "best" weapon for a specific target: some might be more effective than others, but often two or three different types of weapons might be employed against the same target. Additionally, a given weapon might have multiple capabilities: for example, as well as its standard AP projectiles an AT gun might have HE rounds to attack fortifications and exposed troops. Mortars could fire HE or lay smoke screens. Infantry guns were capable of both direct and indirect HE and smoke-laying fire against fortifications, crew-served weapons, and troops in the open, and could deliver direct fire with AT rounds against AFVs (although they were less than adequate for that mission). Some of these weapons were almost identical in design and capabilities between countries, and others were unique. There were also similarities between tactics and employment, and how they were allocated to units.

While doctrine changed during the course of war, other variables were terrain, weather, and evolving enemy tactics. Numbers and allocation evolved and new fire support weapons were fielded, some to replace existing weapons and others to augment them, expanding their capabilities with improved effectiveness. Fire support served to enhance line-company firepower, to gain fire superiority by inflicting more concentrated and accurate fire on the enemy and degrade his own fire. These weapons were allocated to different echelons rather than being evenly distributed at the lowest echelon. This allowed commanders to influence the battlefield by being able to re-allocate and concentrate weapons where they could have the most impact.

The weight and portability of the weapons, their associated equipment, and ammunition was critical. The weapon crew had to keep pace with the infantry unit they supported or follow close behind. To accomplish this, some weapons could be broken down into man-portable loads. Heavier weapons might be carried by pack mules or horses, animal-drawn on their own carriage or in a cart, or towed by light cross-country vehicles. Regardless of weight, it was necessary for all to be manhandled short distances to alternate or supplementary fire positions.

For the most part these weapons did not require excessive ranges. Most targets were at line-of-sight tactical ranges, being detected by frontline infantrymen, but some weapons did have a longer reach, allowing them to support patrols beyond the frontline or engage targets just behind the enemy frontline.

This German 7.92mm MG42 in light configuration, with a three-man "troop" or crew, is fired resting on the shoulder of the assistant gunner – common practice, to provide a relatively stable brace for the gun when firing bursts at longer range. The MG42 weighed 25lb 8oz with its bipod, and its cyclic (i.e. mechanically theoretical) rate of fire was the very high 1,100–1,200rpm that made its sound signature unmistakable. A rifle company initially had nine LMGs, but late in the war that number might be doubled, especially on the Eastern Front. (Tom Laemlein/Armor Plate Press)

Basic infantry unit allocation

The US, Soviet, and German infantry regiments, three to a division, each consisted of three battalions plus various supporting companies under regimental control (though Germany was obliged to change to two-battalion regiments in 1944). The British and Commonwealth division employed three brigades, each with three battalions. They had no organic brigade supporting units; instead these were assigned to the division, and allocated to brigades and battalions as necessary.

In most armies three rifle platoons per company was normal, with three squads (sections) per platoon; some armies began the war with four squads, but with losses and the need to expand armies they soon dropped to three. Infantry battalions consisted of a headquarters company plus three rifle companies (British and Commonwealth, four from 1943), with three rifle platoons per company. Battalions might or might not have a separate weapons or support company; if not, the supporting weapons were assigned to the headquarters company (e.g. in British and Commonwealth battalions pre-1943, when a support company was introduced). Soviet battalions and regiments possessed multiple supporting weapons platoons and companies. This book will cover supporting weapons as they were allotted to "standard" infantry regiments; assignments in parachute, glider, mountain, light, and other specialized regiments were often different.

The smallest tactical unit is the squad in US service, the equivalent "section" in both British Commonwealth and Soviet armies (*otdyelenye*), and the "group" (*Gruppe*) in Germany. For the purposes of this work the term "squad" is used generically when referring to those elements collectively.

When "regiment" is referred to in general terms, this also includes the British and Commonwealth brigade.

Origins of infantry fire support

World War I saw the machine gun drive armies below the ground and created a virtually uncrossable No Man's Land, regardless of determination and esprit de corps. That war also saw the introduction of other supporting weapons to aid the infantry in crossing the deadly ground and breaking into enemy positions.

Many Waffen-SS units were issued high-quality weapons produced in occupied Czechoslovakia, where the Germans kept arms factories in operation throughout the war. The vz26 and externally identical vz30 light machine guns (see left) were often issued in lieu of MG34s, and used the same 7.92x57mm ammunition; in German service they were termed the MG26(t) and MG30(t). Both were fed from 20-rd top-mounted magazines; the vz30 was the weapon from which the British Bren gun was developed. (Tom Laemlein/Armor Plate Press)

The British began the Great War with only two Vickers MGs per battalion. Despite the fact that as late as 1915 Gen Sir Douglas Haig, commanding First British Army, described the machine gun as "a much overrated weapon," this ratio was increased to four guns, subsequently concentrated into an MG company (16x guns) in each brigade; a fourth divisional company was later added, and in 1918 the four companies were consolidated into a divisional battalion. By 1916 each rifle platoon had one Lewis LMG, and by 1918 each section (36 per battalion) had received one. In 1916, brigades received a battery of eight 3in Stokes mortars.

The Germans began the war with 72 machine guns in their division – six per battalion. They later added a divisional MG battalion, an MG company for infantry battalions, and two LMGs per rifle platoon. In 1916 Germany fielded the new type 7.6cm mortar (*Minenwerfer*), six to a regiment. Used until the mid-1930s, this was much heavier and more complex than the Stokes mortar, but it encouraged the development of German infantry guns.

The US fielded only four MGs per infantry regiment in 1916. In France, 1917–18, the division had four regimental MG companies, a three-company MG battalion in both two-regiment brigades, and a two-company divisional MG battalion – a total of 12 companies per division, each with 12x HMGs (plus four spares) of US, British, or French manufacture – enough companies for one per infantry battalion. Rifle platoons had four French-made LMGs, 64 per battalion. Regiments had three French tripod-mounted 37mm M1916 infantry guns, and six 3in Stokes mortars.

Between the wars, machine guns were improved and remained the principal infantry fire support weapon. Through the 1920s and 1930s, improved and lightened mortars became fixtures at company and battalion levels. Heavy "chemical" mortars were fielded for delivering chemical warfare agents and screening smoke; they also fired HE, and were extensively used for fire support.

Light AT guns and AT rifles were fielded in the 1930s, when the rapid future evolution of tank armor was little anticipated. Infantry guns – essentially, miniature field guns – were added by some armies in the 1930s, for the most part owing to the lessons learned in World War I. Prominent among these lessons were two in particular: the inability of even light artillery to move across No Man's Land to support the infantry advance, and the unreliability of communications between the infantry and supporting artillery.

Glossary of relevant terms

The precise meaning of terms varied between languages, and between the tactics and doctrine of different armies:

alternate position	A weapon position covering the same sector as the primary position.
barrage	A concentration of fire on a particular area, point, or line, to cover an advance or halt an attack.
beaten zone	A concentrated MG-fire impact area.
concealment	Hidden from observation, but not necessarily protected from fire.
cover	Protection from fire and usually from observation.
direct fire	Line-of-sight fire directly at a target (*aka* open sights).
direct support	Fire support elements tasked to support a specific maneuver unit.
field (sector) of fire	A sector or fan of fire covered by a specific weapon.
fire and maneuver	Infantry employing movement covered by fire to advance against the enemy.
final defensive fire	Fixed lines of MG fire covering forward positions, and pre-plotted close-in mortar and gun barrages fired as the enemy makes his final assault.
forward observer (FO)	A trained officer in communication with the firing unit, who detects targets and directs and adjusts fire against them. (British = FOO.)
general support	Fire support elements tasked to provide support to more than one maneuver unit.
grazing fire	A line of direct fire aimed just above the ground.
harassing & interdiction fire	Blind firing at possible enemy elements, in hopes of hindering their activities.
indirect fire	Fire directed at a target not visible to the firing unit but directed by FOs; or pre-planned fires on suspected areas of enemy activity.
observed fire	When the impact area can be seen by the weapon crew or by an FO adjusting the fire.
overhead fire	Direct and indirect fire passing over the heads of friendly troops in the open or dug in. Only employed when necessary.
plunging fire	Indirect fire dropping onto a target or area.
primary position	A weapon position covering a specific sector or target area.
reference point (RP)	A recognizable point/feature from which fires are adjusted to other targets (*aka* orientation point).
registration fire	Indirect fire to confirm the weapon is impacting on a reference point, allowing it to be adjusted onto other targets.
rolling barrage	Pre-planned indirect fire barrage that moves forward on a timed schedule ahead of advancing troops (*aka* creeping barrage).
secondary position	A weapon position covering a different sector than the primary and alternate positions.
suppressive fire	Fire directed at known and suspected enemy positions to hinder their return fire (*aka* covering fire).

INFANTRY FIRE SUPPORT WEAPONS

The types and characteristics of fire support weapons varied between countries; while many shared common characteristics and even common roots, there were some unusual and unique weapons.

Basically, at company level crew-served weapons could be transported by one or two men, at least for short distances, while additional men were necessary to carry the ammunition. At battalion level a weapon could generally be manhandled short distances by three or four men, with more for the ammunition. Carts, wagons, or light trucks were available for movement over significant distances. Regimental-level weapons usually demanded the same, but required heavier transport.

Sufficient transport was essential. While many weapons could be manhandled or broken down into one-man loads, this would exhaust the crew crossing rugged terrain; unable to keep pace with the infantry, they were too slow to relocate to new positions. It was essential to reposition weapons whenever their original positions were detected, when the forward troops advanced, and to meet different threats or undertake different missions. Without transport, additional manpower would be necessary to hand-carry ammunition, weapon equipment, and the crew's gear. The quantity and weight of the ammunition was substantial, since crew-served weapons consumed it voraciously. Motor transport was particularly essential for AT guns, which had to be repositioned rapidly and frequently in order to survive.

Machine guns

Rifle-caliber HMGs were primarily to provide long-range indirect fire – over 1,000 yards – and final defensive fires (although, of course, they could also be employed in any other role to include close-range fires, antiaircraft, etc.). They were typically mounted on a heavy tripod to ensure stability for accurate long-range fire to 3,000-plus yards. Only the Germans used an optical sight, though for long-range fire the US and British used clinometers and dial sights, respectively. The US, British, and USSR used water-cooled guns for sustained fire; the Germans used a recoil-absorbing mount for their air-cooled gun, to reduce weight. Rates of fire were in the neighborhood of 450–550rpm, but almost twice as high for German guns. Such weapons were typically manned by relatively large crews, since they frequently had to be man-packed to isolated positions together with large amounts of ammunition.

LMGs were allocated one per rifle squad in most armies, though two in some instances. The concept was developed by the French in World War I and adopted virtually worldwide. Most of these weapons were bipod-mounted

---

A

GERMAN INFANTRY REGIMENT
FIRE SUPPORT IN THE ATTACK, 1940

The allocation and deployment of organic fire support assets was similar to US practices, but it cannot be emphasized enough that such deployment is always dependant on the terrain in both the unit's and the enemy's occupied areas. US tactical symbols are used here; Roman numerals indicate battalions, and Arabic numerals companies.

This shows I and II Battalions in attack positions on fronts of about 100 yards; I Bn (1st–3rd Companies) conducts the main attack, and II Bn (5th–7th Cos) the supporting attack. III Bn (9th–11th Cos) is in reserve, but also tasked to protect the regiment's left flank – an important role for some supporting weapons. Within I Bn, 1st Co is conducting the main attack, with 2nd Co providing covering fire, and 3rd Co in reserve. Detailed here are the positioning and missions of each battalion MG company's 12x HMGs and 6x 8cm mortars (4th, 8th and 12th Cos); plus the 4x 7.5cm and 2x 15cm guns of the regimental infantry-gun company (13th Co); and the 12x 3.7cm guns of the regimental AT company (14th Co). From 1942 the 13th Co began rearming with 8x 12cm heavy mortars, which were deployed similarly to the infantry guns they replaced, or were centralized.

Note that in most cases the support weapons were deployed in pairs (sections, half-platoons) or fours (platoons).

The mission of each lettered, circled group is identified. The HMG platoons (see key panel) are *not* lettered; they provide support to the infantry company to which they are adjacent. The infantry companies' organic AT rifles (x3), platoon 5cm mortars (one each), and squad LMGs (one each – nine per company) are not indicated. Subunit missions:

(a) Covering fire for 1st Company's main attack.

(b) Covering fire for 2nd Co's supporting attack.

(c) Protects flank; will support 3rd Co when it advances.

(d) Protects flank; will support 9th Co when it advances.

(e) Indirect fire support to 1st Co; will accompany its advance.

(f) Indirect fire support to 1st Co; secondary to 2nd Co, and to II Bn if needed.

(g) Supports 1st and 2nd Cos (each symbol = 3x mortars) .

(h) Covering fire for 5th Co.

(i) Covering fire for 6th Co.

(j) Supports 7th Co when it advances.

(k) Supports 5th Co (each symbol = one mortar).

(l) Supports 6th Co (each symbol = one mortar).

(m) Supports 7th Co when it advances (each symbol = one mortar).

(n) Indirect fire support for 5th and 6th Cos.

(o) Regimental pioneer ptn – supports main attack by obstacle-breaching and mine-clearance.

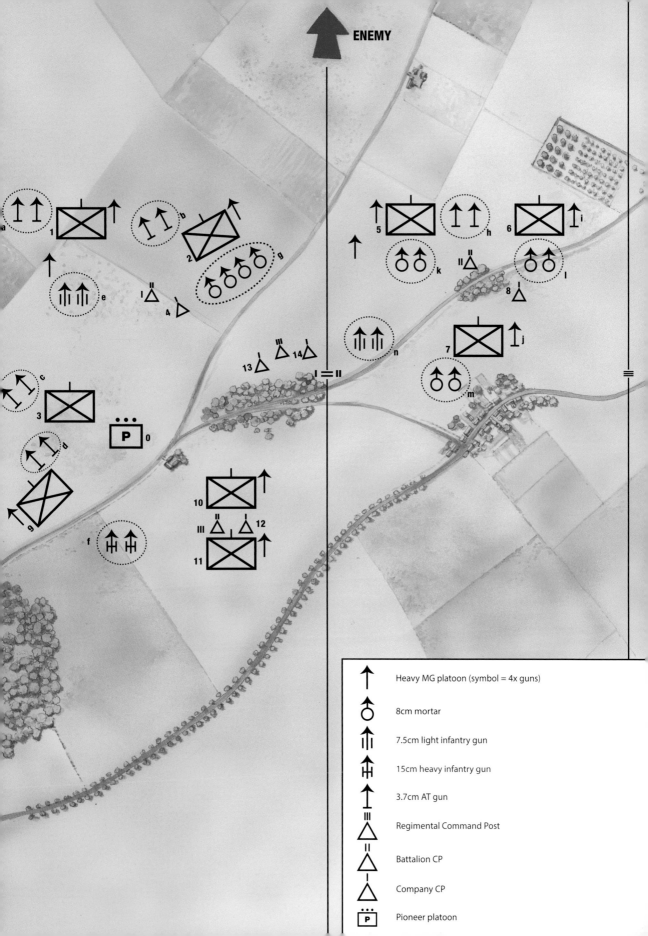

ENEMY

Heavy MG platoon (symbol = 4x guns)

8cm mortar

7.5cm light infantry gun

15cm heavy infantry gun

3.7cm AT gun

Regimental Command Post

Battalion CP

Company CP

Pioneer platoon

Weapons nomenclature, with (contemporary abbreviations)

English	German	Russian
machine gun (MG)	Maschinengewehr (MG)	Pulemyot
mortar (mort *or* mor)	Granatwerfer (GrW)	Minomyot
infantry gun (inf gun)	Infanterie-Geschütz (IG)	Polkovaya Pushka
antitank gun (AT* gun)	Panzer-abwher-Kanone (PaK)	Protivotankovaya Pushka
antitank rifle (AT* rfl)	Panzerbüchse (PzB)	Protivotankovoye Ruzhye
light (lt)	leichtes (l *or* le)	*(Weight classes not*
medium (med *or* md)	mittlerer (m *or* mittl)	*used by USSR to*
heavy (hv)	schwere (s *or* schw)	*designate weapons.)*

(* British, "anti-tank (A Tk)")

and magazine-fed using rifle ammunition, although the Germans used heavier belt-fed weapons. Essentially the LMG was the lowest-level fire support weapon, though rifle squads were also usually equipped with at least one rifle-grenade launcher. Most armies organized their rifle squads into a rifle group under the squad leader and an LMG group under the assistant squad leader.

"Light", "medium", and "heavy" machine guns

There seems to be a common impression that there are hard and fast definitions for each category of "small arms" – weapons under 15mm (.59cal) – and some people puzzle over whether a particular model of machine gun is heavy, medium, light, or general-purpose. There is a popular tendency to use the term "light machine guns" only for bipod-mounted guns fired from the hip or shoulder; "medium machine guns" are viewed as tripod-mounted air-cooled guns; while "heavy machine guns" are tripod-mounted water-cooled guns or those of larger than rifle caliber. Such attempted definitions are of little value.

A section of the 3rd Greek Mtn Bde in Italy, equipped by the British and under I Canadian Corps, secures a bridge construction site. The light machine-gunner is armed with a .303in Mk I Bren gun. Weighing 23lb and fed by 30-rd curved box magazines (the shape required by the rimmed British .303in round), the Bren had a cyclic rate of 540rpm. By comparison the equivalent US squad LMG, the .30cal M1918A2 BAR, weighed only 19lb 6oz with a 20-rd mag, and had a rate of 300–450rpm, but the need to change magazines frequently after only 4–6 short bursts limited the BAR's sustained-fire capability. The Bren was, if anything, *too* accurate: unless a gunner consciously moved his shoulder, its shot groups were too close to be effective against area targets and small groups of personnel. Typically, the rifle section's six riflemen each carried two Bren magazines, the LMG group leader and the No. 1 gunner four each, and the No. 2 eight, giving the section a total of 28 spare mags plus one on the gun when they first went into combat. (Tom Laemlein/Armor Plate Press)

For instance, the British called their water-cooled .303in Mk I Vickers a "medium machine gun," while the US called their water-cooled .30cal M1917A1 Browning a "heavy machine gun." Both were virtually identical in general description, capabilities, and role, and both weighed about 42lbs with a full water-jacket.

In US doctrine the terms "light" and "heavy" machine guns more accurately defined their roles rather than their physical weight. The HMG, the M1917A1, was a battalion-level weapon providing long-range fire on point and area targets. This required a high degree of accuracy, and both direct and indirect fire over the heads of friendly troops, and the M1917A1's heavy weight and robust tripod provided the necessary stability. LMGs, the M1919 series, were company-level weapons; they were required to be highly mobile in order to keep up with infantrymen, and were employed for short-range suppressive fires. The terms "heavy" and "light" were not part of the American guns' designations, but rather identified the subunits to which they were organic – HMG platoons in the battalion weapons company, and LMG squads in the rifle company's weapons platoon. (The term "medium MG" was never used in US practice.)

What most armies referred to as "light machine guns" were in fact the forerunners of today's "squad automatic weapons" – i.e. bipod-mounted, fired from shoulder or hip, and usually magazine-fed. The US referred to its squad automatic weapon, the BAR, as an "automatic rifle," as distinct from the "light machine gun" allocated at company level.

The German 7.92mm MG34 and MG42 machine guns were used in both the light (*leicht*) and heavy (*schwere*) roles – terms that had nothing to do with the guns' weight, but referred to different roles, accessories and crews. MGs in the light role were assigned to rifle squads and were fired only from the shoulder or bipod, by a three-man crew provided with five "basket" magazines with 50-rd belts, two 250-rd belts in boxes, and two spare barrels. In the heavy role the same guns were used for long-range, sustained supporting fire, and were assigned to battalion MG companies. A six-man crew was provided a recoil-damping tripod with a feature allowing it to traverse back and forth at set ranges (*Tiefenfeuerautomat*), a long-range optical sight graduated to 3,830 yards, numerous 250-rd belts in boxes, and three spare barrels.

France, 1944: in dense woodland, US .30cal M1917A1 heavy machine guns cannot provide long-range supporting fire from the rear or in gaps separating forward units. Instead, they have been positioned with forward rifle platoons to give direct close-range support. A rifle company (i.e. its two platoons that were deployed forward) typically had six integral M1918A2 BARs and two M1919A4 LMGs, plus possibly an attached two-gun section or four-gun platoon of M1917A1 HMGs. With 60-plus M1 semi-automatic rifles, that added up to a considerable amount of automatic firepower. (Tom Laemlein/Armor Plate Press)

Mortars

Mortars were the infantryman's "pocket artillery." They were cheap to make, simple to operate, reasonably accurate, lightweight and portable, but delivered relatively powerful HE and effective smoke rounds. Though mainly indirect-fire weapons, in World War II they most often engaged targets within visual

range of the crew; they were seldom directed by FOs other than for on-call fires requested by company/platoon commanders. They were fired at high angles of 40–85 degrees. Most combatant armies used Brandt-type mortars of 81mm (3.2in) caliber weighing 100lb-plus, allocated at regimental level.[1] Maximum ranges were 2,600 to 3,000-plus yards, with a rate of fire of 15–25rpm over short periods.

On the eve of World War II many countries also developed light, simple mortars to replace or supplement rifle-grenade launchers at platoon level; some could be employed for direct as well as indirect fire. These light mortars included Brandt types, but several other innovative and usually complex designs were also found. They were typically of 50mm (1.9in) or 60mm (2.3in) caliber, light enough to be carried by one man. Their range varied, but was less than 1,000 yards; with a two-man crew, they were often allocated one per rifle platoon.

A US 60mm M2 mortar gunner and assistant gunner relax in their hastily dug position, consisting of two prone foxholes doubling as sleeping trenches. The rifle company's weapons platoon possessed a section with three 60mm mortars. In the defense these were laid for preplanned barrages on infantry avenues of approach, and (after these became available in 1944) fired parachute-suspended illumination flares. They were usually kept together as a section under company control, seldom being attached individually to rifle platoons. The M2 weighed 42lb, and with a 28.6in barrel it fired a 3lb HE round out to between 100 and 1,935 yards. (Tom Laemlein/Armor Plate Press)

At the opposite end of the spectrum were heavy mortars of 4.2in (107mm) or 120mm (4.7in) caliber. With ranges of 4,000–6,000 yards, these threw artillery-weight projectiles at higher rates than artillery, delivering both HE and smoke (for which most were originally developed). In some instances they were assigned at infantry regimental level, but they were more often divisional assets that were frequently attached to regiments. This class of mortar required artillery-size crews and motor transport.

Infantry guns

This category of guns was born in World War I to meet the need for a man-handlable support weapon that could accompany advancing infantry across the wire-entangled, cratered sea of mud in No Man's Land. Directing distant artillery by the means of communication then available was extremely difficult. The concept of "accompanying artillery" attached to infantry for direct support did not really work, however; although the German Army was still using them in 1918, the guns could seldom negotiate the battlefield and keep pace with infantry. From 1916, the Germans used a 7.6cm mortar on a two-wheel carriage with a large 360-degree turntable base and trail. It was dismounted from the wheels and set on the ground for indirect or direct

1 Edgar Brandt (1880–1960) had his first 60mm breech-loading pneumatic mortar accepted by the French Army in 1916, and thereafter designed a series of muzzle-loading mortars between 60mm and 120mm, up to 1935. The basic design consisted of a barrel with a fixed firing pin; a relatively heavy, variously shaped baseplate; an adjustable-height bipod, with a traversing mechanism and one or two small recoil cylinders; and a collimator sight. With slight adaptations, Brandt's mortars were produced under license by many countries, and the 81mm practically became a worldwide standard. Brandt was also responsible for the streamlined, teardrop-shaped mortar bomb. Most countries produced HE and smoke rounds; Britain also produced parachute-suspended illumination rounds for its 2in mortar, and the US introduced equivalents in 60mm and 81mm early in 1944. Honored as a Knight of the Legion of Honor in 1939, Brandt moved permanently to Switzerland before the outbreak of World War II. His nearly 90-year-old design remains in wide use throughout the world, with little change.

Despite its shorter 46in barrel, the Red Army's 76mm M1927 "regimental gun" – actually a howitzer – had a longer range (9,350 yards) than any of the German infantry guns, and, at 14rpm, a higher rate of fire with its 13lb 11oz HE round. The Germans employed captured guns as the 7.62cm IKH290(r). A lightened and improved M1943 version was subsequently fielded, with a much modified M1927 barrel mated to the carriage and shield of the 45mm M1942 AT gun. (Tom Laemlein/Armor Plate Press)

firing, the latter for anti-pillbox and marginal AT use. The Germans also employed obsolescent hand-drawn 7.7cm field guns assigned to "infantry batteries," allotted one gun per battalion.

Many countries abandoned the infantry-gun concept after the Great War and relied on mortars, but Germany further developed the *Infantrie-Geschütze*, which was essentially a miniature 7.5cm artillery piece that could be broken down into man-packed loads. Fielded in 1929, it could provide direct fire against troops and pillboxes as well as indirect fire. In 1938 they developed a larger 15cm infantry gun to subdue strongpoints and breach barbed wire.

The US essentially copied the concept, but using pack artillery pieces. Initially the 75mm pack howitzer, designed for mule transport and airborne use, was fielded in infantry regiment cannon companies, and in 1943 it was replaced with the 105mm M3 lightweight howitzer. Howitzers provided longer range than mortars and supplemented divisional artillery, as well as providing direct assault fire against enemy positions. The Russians used the 76mm M1927 and the upgraded M1943 infantry guns (commonly called "regimental guns") for short-range support. The British and Commonwealth armies did not possess weapons of this type.

Antitank guns

Most armies began the war with a 37mm AT gun (British and Commonwealth, 2-pdr/40mm). By 1941 these were essentially obsolete, but were often retained: their larger-caliber replacements were slow to arrive, and the light guns remained useful against lightly armored and soft-skin vehicles, field fortifications, buildings, and personnel. In the mid-war they were replaced in the infantry AT role by 50mm and 57mm guns; these typically had artillery-type carriages (two wheels, split trails, and shields to protect from tank MG fire and mortar and artillery fragmentation). Larger-caliber guns were introduced – the US 3in, British 17-pdr (76mm), and German 7.5cm and 8.8cm – but were so large and heavy that they were impractical for infantry use, and mainly equipped divisional or non-

The German 3.7cm PaK35/36 antitank gun was copied or license-built by Italy, the US and the Netherlands. It weighed 723lb, with a 65.5in barrel; its 1lb 8oz AP round had a penetration of 38mm (1.5in) at 400 yards, and a rate of 8–18rpm was achievable. (For comparison, the figures for the US 37mm M3A1 copy were 912lb; 70in; 1lb 15oz; 2.4in/69mm at 500 yards, and 15–20rpm.) German *Panzerabwehr* ("anti-armor") units were first raised in 1934, but to mask their defensive nature in an army geared completely for the offensive they were redesignated *Panzerjäger* ("armor-hunter") on 1 April 1940. (Tom Laemlein/ Armor Plate Press)

The British 2-pdr (40mm) Mk IX antitank gun saw wide use in France in 1940 and in North Africa until mid-1942. It weighed a heavy 1,848lb; as well as a frontal shield it had detachable side-armor plates, though these were little used. Its 2lb 6oz AP shot penetrated 2in (50mm) of armor at 500 yards, and it could be fired at the high rate of 20rpm. Although it was more than twice as heavy as the equivalent German PaK35/36, and its high shield made it hard to conceal in the desert, the more complex mount with easily removable wheels allowed it to traverse 360 degrees. (Tom Laemlein/Armor Plate Press)

divisional AT units. Their size made them difficult to dig in and conceal, and almost impossible to reposition by manhandling once they revealed their position, which was crucial for survival; repositioning by prime-movers was too slow, and provided tempting targets.

The AT gun had a high-speed breech, optical sight, and a comparatively long barrel to attain higher velocity and accuracy. As the enemy's armor improved, longer barrels were provided to increase velocity and penetration. A key factor was that the gun had to have a reasonable degree of traverse in order to track a moving AFV; many had a free-traversing system, which the gunner moved by pressing his shoulder against a support rather than manipulating a slower traversing wheel.

To summarize: small-caliber, lightweight guns that were practical for infantry use became increasingly inadequate as the war progressed; and heavier, large-caliber guns were not sufficiently mobile, and so were easily overrun by tanks if used in the frontline. For the most part towed AT guns were increasingly relegated to secondary roles, and sometimes not even employed. Advances in rocket and recoilless weapons were rendering conventional AT guns obsolete by the war's end.

Shoulder-fired antitank weapons

The capability of infantry to defend themselves against tanks was crucial. Just prior to World War II most countries adopted AT rifle grenades – their first shaped-charge munition – but these achieved only limited penetration and were inaccurate at all but the closest ranges.

The Soviet 14.5mm Degtyarov PTRD-41, the main Red Army antitank rifle throughout the war, was a single-shot, bolt-action weapon weighing 38lb and measuring an unwieldy 78.7in long. The alternative Simonov PTRS-41 semi-automatic, with a 5-rd magazine, was even heavier at 46lb; the barrels were detachable from both weapons to make them more man-portable. The massive 14.5x114mm (.57cal) cartridge used an AP-incendiary bullet with a tungsten-carbide core, but could only penetrate 25mm (0.98in) of armor at 500 yards. (Tom Laemlein/Armor Plate Press)

An M9 or M9A1 bazooka is aimed at a suspect building by a soldier from the US 44th Inf Div during street-fighting outside a German Police hospital in Manheim, spring 1945. Some units trained three or four two-man bazooka teams for attachment to rifle platoons, but usually rifle companies had no dedicated bazooka crewmen; most members of a rifle squad were trained to operate it when necessary. A crew usually carried six or nine rockets, in 3-rd M6 rocket-carrying bags. (Tom Laemlein/Armor Plate Press)

Another prewar weapon was the AT rifle, adopted by all armies except the US. Calibers varied greatly, from the German 7.92mm backed by a massive cartridge case, via the British .55in (13.9mm) and Soviet 14.5mm, to several countries (including Germany) trying 20mm. Heavier than many MGs, these weapons were burdensome to carry owing to their weight and length, and had poor armor penetration and marginal behind-armor effects. Common characteristics were exceedingly long barrels for high velocity, range, and accuracy, and use of a bipod. They might be single-shot or magazine-fed, bolt-action or semi-automatic. By 1942 they were largely withdrawn, though the Red Army continued to use them since little else was available. Their simple "iron sights" made them ill-suited for sniping, but they were sometimes used like (and can be considered the predecessors of) today's large-caliber anti-materiel rifles.

In the mid-war years AT rifles and light AT guns were mostly replaced with new weapons. The US fielded the lightweight 2.36in AT rocket launcher ("bazooka") in late 1942, and improved models were introduced in 1944. It proved to be a relatively effective AT weapon, and also useful against personnel, buildings, and field fortifications. The British fielded the "projector, infantry, antitank" (PIAT) in mid-1943. While heavy, more difficult to use, and shorter-ranged, it was useful in the same range of tactical contexts. The Germans fielded two man-portable AT weapons in 1943: the revolutionary single-shot *Panzerfaust* AT projector was issued in huge numbers, and the bazooka-based 8.8cm *Panzerschreck* rocket launcher actually replaced regimental AT guns. (See commentary to Plate H.)

FIRE SUPPORT WEAPONS' EFFECTS

The variety of fire support weapons provided a wide range of capabilities and means of attacking different types of targets. While there is little mention of supporting weapons in wartime accounts, which may suggest underutilization, their effective employment reinforced a unit's combat power. A commander and staff who were not completely familiar with the capabilities, limitations, and effects of the different weapons and ammunition were limiting their ability to influence the action.

The Russian 7.62mm DP Degtyarev light machine gun was distributed one or two guns per squad; its 47-rd pan magazine gave rise to the nickname *proigryvatel'* ("record-player"). Its operating spring was coiled around the under-barrel operating rod; this caused rapid heating and distortion, leading to malfunctions. From 1943 the DP was replaced by the DPM, with the recoil spring relocated to a tubular housing protruding from the rear of the receiver, and other improvements. The DP had a noticeably long 50in barrel and weighed 23lb 4oz; the cyclic rate was 500–600rpm, though this could be increased to 1,000–1,200rpm for AA use. (Tom Laemlein/Armor Plate Press)

Light and heavy machine guns

The high rate of fire generated by MGs, coupled with their reasonable range, made them effective anti-personnel weapons. Bipod-mounted LMGs, typically weighing three times or more than a rifle, were still light enough for squad machine-gunners to keep up with riflemen. LMGs were also effective when in close combat in forests and urban areas, and clearing field fortifications. While the same caliber as rifles, they assured hits on man-size targets at longer than rifle ranges. Using a short burst, they could knock down a moving man when that might require numerous rifle shots, and they were effective against crew-served weapons or clumped troops.

Their main benefit was to provide the squad with a base of fire, delivering repeated suppressive-fire bursts to force the enemy to keep their heads down as the squad's riflemen maneuvered. A measure of an LMG's effectiveness was the number of successive bursts it could deliver before reloading. The US BAR was the least capable, with only a 20-rd magazine (four to five short bursts). The British Bren had a 30-rd magazine, and the Soviet DP and DPM

B | **GERMAN INFANTRY REGIMENT**
FIRE SUPPORT IN DEFENSE, 1944

The New Type German infantry regiment of 1944 had only two battalions. The battalion machine-gun companies (4th and 8th) were reorganized as "heavy companies," with two HMG platoons (four guns each); an 8cm mortar platoon (six tubes); and a 7.5cm infantry-gun platoon (four guns). The regimental infantry-gun company (13th) had one gun platoon (either 4x 7.5cm, or two each 7.5cm and 15cm), and two heavy mortar platoons (each 4x 12cm tubes). The 14th Co was now a "tank destroyer" company; instead of AT guns it had 54x *Panzerschreck* rocket launchers, in three platoons of 18 each. Due to shortages units seldom possessed their full allocation of weapons, and most regiments' heavy, infantry-gun, and tank-destroyer companies had fewer weapons in different mixes, simply as available.

In the defense, fire support weapons are deployed in depth, positioned to protect flanks and to cover avenues for Allied tank advances running through the unit's sector. Roadblocks of interlocking felled trees and small minefields block the roads, and are covered by LMGs, HMGs, and *Panzerschrecks*. Mortar and infantry-gun concentrations are plotted in front of or on these obstacles, and a battery of four

7.5cm-armed SP armored assault guns are attached in support. The 7th Company and the pioneer platoon (with 6x LMG) form the regimental reserve in and around a village. The missions of lettered, circled groups of weapons are identified below; as on Plate A, the HMG platoons are *not* lettered, as they simply support the adjacent infantry companies (1st and 2nd, 5th and 6th). The 14th Co's *Panzerschrecks* are not indicated; the company's 18 "troops" each of three two-man crews were scattered in depth throughout the defensive sector, deployed to cover tank approach-avenues with interlocking fire. Additionally, each rifle company was authorized up to 36 *Panzerfauste*, and the 14th Co had 90 in addition to its *Panzerschrecks*. Subunit missions:

(a) Supports 1st and 2nd Cos.
(b) Supports 5th and 6th Cos.
(c) Supports 7th Co (regimental reserve).
(d) Supports 1st and 2nd Companies.
(e) Supports 5th and 6th Cos.
(f) Supports regimental reserve.
(g) Supports I Battalion; secondary support to II Bn.
(h) Supports I Bn.
(i) Supports II Bn..

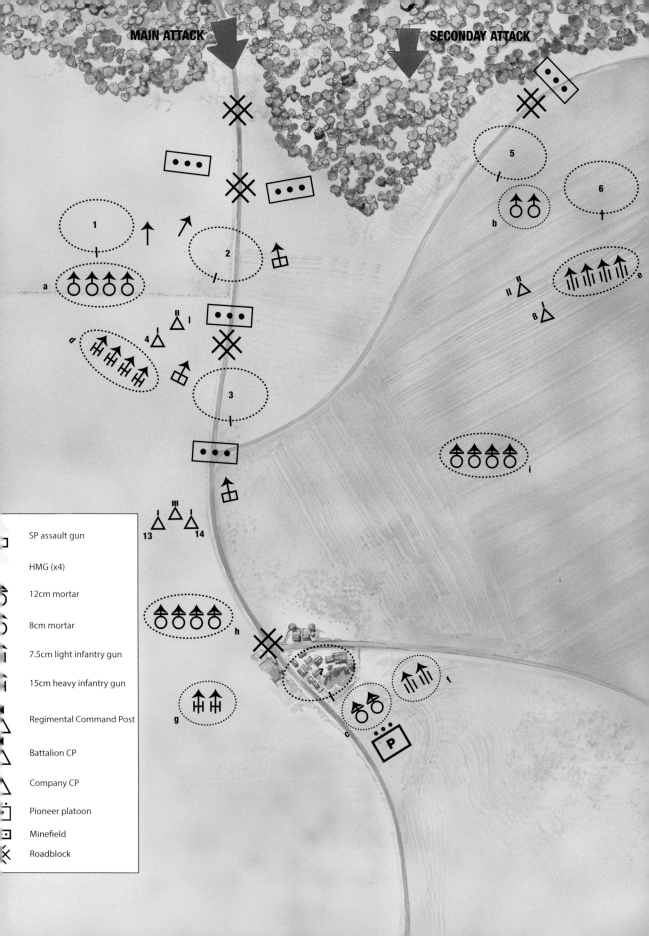

MAIN ATTACK

SECONDAY ATTACK

1

2

3

4

5

6

7

8

13

14

a

b

c

d

e

f

g

h

i

P

SP assault gun	
HMG (x4)	
12cm mortar	
8cm mortar	
7.5cm light infantry gun	
15cm heavy infantry gun	
Regimental Command Post	
Battalion CP	
Company CP	
Pioneer platoon	
Minefield	
Roadblock	

The crew of a US .30cal M1917A1 heavy machine gun maintain a high rate of long-range fire while covering the advance of their infantry near Schlich, Germany, December 1944; this gun is fitted with an M1923 flash-hider. The M1917A1 and its tripod weighed 83lb 10oz plus 6–8lb for water. Fed with 250-rd belts, its cyclic rate was 450–600rpm, but like all MGs its practical rate was far lower, around 150rpm. At that rate, and filled with seven pints of water, the gun would steam after two to three minutes, and would overheat in five. Gun positions were commonly littered with empty ammo cans and web feed belts. See Plate D. (Tom Laemlein/Armor Plate Press)

47-rd pans. The MG34 and MG42 were the most capable, with a 50-rd belt in a "basket" magazine plus additional belts that could be linked together. The Bren was considered the most accurate, but this was not necessarily a benefit: LMGs were intended for small area targets and groups of personnel, and precise accuracy was unnecessary. In the defense, LMGs could hold their automatic fire so as not to reveal their position, firing only single shots until the enemy was closer. Most LMGs fired 450–550rpm, while the German guns famously spit out twice that; while wasteful, this did assure more hits at long ranges. For longer-range engagements longer bursts were required, owing to natural bullet-spread, and most LMGs were capable of rapid barrel changes when they overheated.

Heavy MGs, usually at battalion-level on heavy tripods, provided long-range direct and indirect fire. The US Browning, British Vickers, and Russian Maxim were water-cooled. Being belt-fed meant they could maintain prolonged but not continuous fire, and replacing overheated barrels was tricky and time-consuming. The Germans relied on quick-change barrels (10–15 seconds) for their air-cooled weapons. While HMGs could of course be used at the shortest ranges, they were intended for long range; using a clinometer or dial sight and a firing table to determine the angle of elevation, they could be employed for indirect fires at over 3,000 yards. Fire could be directed over ridges and tree lines with a plunging effect, but this still fell at a relatively shallow trajectory. Indirect fire skills, perfected in World War I, deteriorated through World War II owing to wider use of artillery and mortars and the realities of mobile warfare. HMGs still proved valuable for direct long-range supporting and suppressive fires, though in rough and close terrain they were difficult to move forward.

MGs used the same ammunition as rifles, but special-purpose rounds were available. AP had little effect on AFVs, but improved penetration through soft-skin vehicles, aircraft, and typical cover materials: masonry, concrete, logs, sandbags, foxhole parapets, etc. There were combination rounds such as AP-tracer or AP-incendiary, but these were mainly for AA use.

Streams of fire: tracers

All armies provided tracers for machine guns, typically every fifth round in a belt. Tracers allowed the gunner to correct his aim at long range where bullet impact was not visible. Fire could even be adjusted by "sensing" the tracer burst

A German 7.92mm MG34 from the battalion machine-gun company in the heavy role, on the recoil-absorbing tripod mount (*Lafette 34* – as also used with the MG42), complete with the 1.5x *Zielfernrohr 40* optical collimator sight. Together with the tripod the MG34 weighed about 69lb; it was fed with 50-rd or 250-rd belts, and had a cyclic rate of 800–900rpm. While the MG42 was manufactured from 1942 to replace the MG34, the latter remained in production until the war's end. Gun crews (of six or seven men in the HMG role) were also provided with an antiaircraft tripod – the *Dreibein 34* – from which the gunner could fire from the crouching or standing position. (Tom Laemlein/Armor Plate Press)

and making corrections before the rounds impacted. For AA use, tracers were useful in correcting aim when firing at a high-speed aircraft. They could also ignite fuel, and had a psychological effect on pilots – and not only on pilots:

"German prisoners attributed the failure of their attack on Bastogne, Belgium on the morning of 30 December 1944 in large part to the lavish expenditure of tracer bullets by the defending 101st Airborne Division. All prisoners questioned stated that the illumination caused by the tracers made every soldier feel that he could go no further without being spotted and that the morale was lowered considerably because every tracer bullet looked as if it were coming right at you. Even enemy troops who had already seen five years of combat, including the Stalingrad battle, commented that the display was more frightening than anything they had experienced previously" (*Intelligence Bulletin*, 1945).

The incendiary effects could set soft-skin vehicles, wooden structures, and vegetation alight. Frontline troops frequently designated targets for mortars, infantry guns, and tanks by firing tracers (a single tracer stream directly at the target or, better, two intersecting streams), and the flanks of a target area might be marked by two machine guns. A German trick was to fire MG bursts with tracers deceptively high overhead to lure in patrols probing the lines, while other guns fired tracerless bursts just above ground level.

Patrols operating forward of their lines at night would arrange for a machine gun in their unit's sector to fire long bursts of tracers along a given azimuth at specified times, or on call, at a hilltop or other dominant terrain feature unoccupied by friendly forces. This feature was *not* the patrol's objective, merely a reference point that could be identified from most points in the area. This allowed patrols to confirm their own location and direction of movement. Another technique was to fire an occasional burst at a high angle to give patrols a reference point for night navigation.

It is often said that "tracers work both ways," meaning the enemy might be able to locate a machine gun by its tracer stream. This can occur, but when multiple weapons are firing, including rifles without tracers, it is difficult to determine MG locations, and this also depends on the angle of view. In one engagement, a US quad-.50cal AA MG battery tasked with supporting an infantry attack planned to remove the tracers to reduce the possibility of their firing positions being detected as they placed suppressive fire on the objective. Learning of this, the infantry requested they use tracer, as it had a good effect on own-troops' morale and would further demoralize the enemy; the AA unit granted this request, deciding it was worth the risk.

Both US and Commonwealth forces used mostly red tracers, although the US used some green tracers early in the war. The Germans used tracers that first burned red and then green (sometimes described as greenish-white), or the reverse. The Red Army used red tracers, but some first burned red and then green. (Soviet all-green tracers were a postwar practice.)

Mortars

Reports revealed that troops often feared enemy mortars but discounted their own, possibly because of the bursts appearing smaller than artillery shells. Incoming mortar rounds were silent as opposed to whistling artillery, and mortars caused huge numbers of casualties on both sides. They could deliver great amounts of indirect firepower for their weight; ammunition consumption was high owing to their marginal accuracy, demanding that heavy loads be carried. Most mortars, except the heaviest, could be broken down into two to four man-packed loads. Their high-angle fire was beneficial in that they could reach targets that were in defilade or dead zones – behind hills and ridges, in ravines, covered by tree lines or buildings, etc.

BRITISH INFANTRY BATTALION IN THE ATTACK, 1944

British and Commonwealth infantry battalions had four rifle companies, unlike the three of most other wartime armies. While the battalion's and brigade's organic fire support assets were more limited than in other armies, four rifle companies gave the unit great tactical flexibility.

Here, A and B Companies are positioned behind or on their lines-of-departure (LD) to conduct the main attack on a village (here generically named Kleinstadt), supported by an attached troop of three Churchill tanks. To the right rear, C Co is in reserve preparing to support the main attack; meanwhile, at Bauernhof beyond the right flank, D Co will execute a supporting attack through a small wood and on to take a defended farm. Just prior to the main attack plentiful artillery will barrage the village and the large Große Wald wood, to "shoot" the main attack companies onto the objective. Sapper sections from the battalion HQ Co's pioneer platoon will breach the roadblocks.

The infantry battalion relied mainly upon its Support Co's organic AT platoon (6x 6-pdr), mortar platoon (6x 3in), and carrier platoon. The latter was 58 strong, with 13x Universal tracked "Bren gun" carriers with four-man crews, in four sections each of three carriers (plus a section with 12 motorcycles for recon and dispatch riders). Each of the carrier sections had 3x Bren LMGs, a 2in mortar, and a PIAT, giving the carrier platoon more firepower in those weapons than a rifle company. The carrier platoon could conduct reconnaissance, protect flanks, provide close fire support, serve as a mobile reserve, add depth to the defense, and haul supplies forward and casualties to the rear. Here it is divided, to both support the main attack and reinforce C Co in the reserve role. Other carriers transported the Support Co's 3in mortars, and the Vickers MMGs attached from the division's machine-gun battalion. The 6-pdr AT guns were towed by heavier Loyd TT carriers, each accompanied by a second carrier with

ammunition, a 2in mortar for smoke and illumination, and a Bren for close defense.

Here the infantry section Bren LMGs (x9 per company), 2in mortars and PIATs (x3 each per company) are not indicated. US tactical symbols are used. Subunit missions:

(a) A Company, tasked to seize left portion of village, behind line-of-departure.

(b) B Co, tasked to seize right portion of village, on line-of-departure.

(c) Tank troop to accompany A Co's attack.

(d) Advanced 6-pdr AT gun section supporting A Co.

(e) 6-pdr AT gun section supporting B Co.

(f) Attached MMG section supporting B Co's attack.

(g) Two 3in mortar sections supporting A and B Cos' attacks.

(h) Section detached from carrier platoon with ammunition, to follow main attack, and then provide fire support in the event of a counterattack.

(i) C Co, prepared to support main attack, and to reinforce in the event of a counterattack.

(j) 6-pdr AT gun section supporting B Co's attack.

(k) Attached MMG section covering Große Wald on right flank of main attack.

(l) Remaining three sections of carrier platoon as mobile reserve attached to C Co.

(m) D Co, tasked to conduct supporting attack on Bauernhof Farm; will then clear Große Wald.

(n) Attached MMG section supporting D Co's initial attack on small wood; will then displace in carriers to support its attack on Bauernhof Farm.

(o) 3in mortar section supporting D Co's attack.

(p) Battalion command post.

(q) Artillery observation post. Apart from the British and Commonwealth, all the armies discussed in this book used a triangle (with various enclosures) as a tactical map symbol for an observation post..

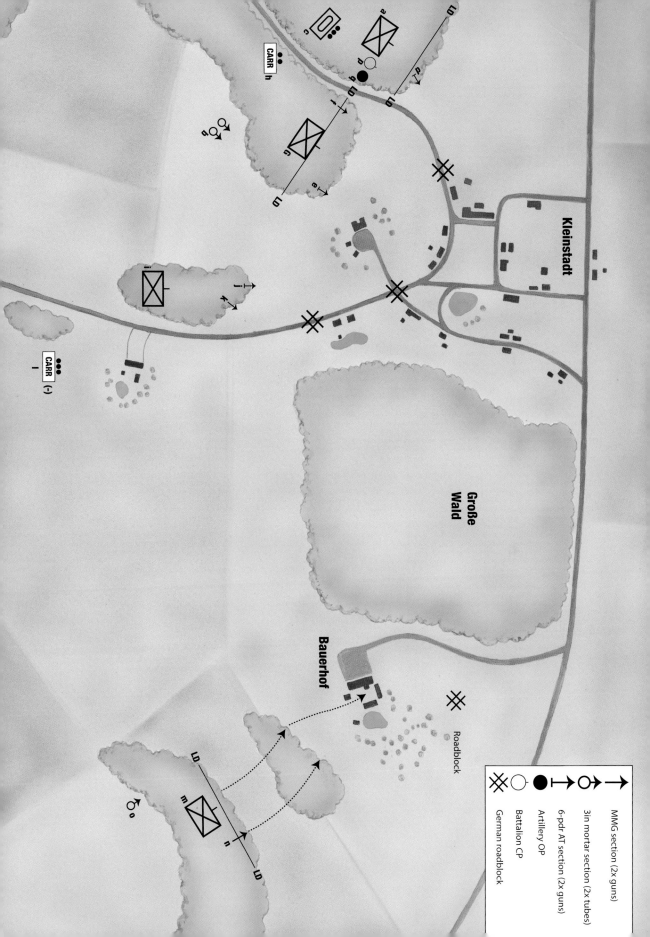

Kleinstadt

Große
Wald

Bauerhof

Roadblock

CARR

CARR (-)

MMG section (2x guns)

3in mortar section (2x tubes)

6-pdr AT section (2x guns)

Artillery OP

Battalion CP

German roadblock

Mortars are viewed as a form of light artillery, but mortar and artillery projectiles are constructed entirely differently. Artillery shells have thick walls, to resist the high forces of firing and to create large destructive fragments with a relatively small bursting charge. Mortar bombs have comparatively thin walls, creating numerous small fragments, and a relatively larger bursting charge for heavy blast effects. Besides deadly anti-personnel effects, the heavy blast is useful for attacking buildings and field fortifications and breaching obstacles. The angle of impact affects casualty radius; since mortar rounds typically impact at a steeper trajectory than artillery shells they therefore detonate with a more uniform blast and fragmentation radius. (Artillery projectiles impacting at shallower angles spray a less uniform casualty pattern: much of the blast and fragmentation is thrown forward in the direction of flight, and some to the sides, little being blown back toward the direction of flight.)

Mortar rounds with instantaneously detonating fuzes make virtually no crater on hard ground, and two layers of sandbags are all that is required to provide overhead protection. Few mortar rounds in World War II had delay-impact fuzes that allowed the round to penetrate overhead cover and burst inside a bunker. Multiple hits were required to neutralize a bunker, which was usually achieved by collapsing the sides, but multiple hits were difficult to achieve owing to the naturally wide dispersion of rounds. While ill-suited for point targets, mortars were effective area-fire weapons. For example, when the US 30th Inf Div breached the Siegfried Line near Aachen, 4.2in mortars of the 92nd Chemical Bn worked over the dense wire entanglements; when the infantry attacked they had no need for bangalore torpedoes and wire-cutters, as the mortars had torn open gaps. They then laid a rolling barrage in front of the advancing troops.

The Germans relied heavily on mortars in the defense, since they were more responsive than artillery and easier to control via poor communications, and they would also support German counterattacks. There were instances when Allied mortars fired on German positions only for the Germans to quickly send a couple of rounds back into Allied positions. This resulted in

Red Army soldiers fire a 1lb 14oz HE bomb from an RM-41, the final design of four Soviet 50mm light mortars (RM-38, RM-39, RM-40, and RM-41). The RM-41 eliminated the earlier models' bipod, being fixed on a large baseplate. It could be set at only two elevations, 45 and 75 degrees; gas vents were used to otherwise adjust the range between its minimum of 50 and maximum of 875 yards. The complete 22lb mortar could be man-packed by a single soldier using a tubular frame. The Germans made use of captured examples of all four models, and even produced their own sight for them. They called the Russian 50mm the *Kartoffel-Werfer* ("potato projector"), believing that rounds in the air looked like lobbed potatoes. (Tom Laemlein/Armor Plate Press)

A British 3in Mk II mortar being fired from a hastily dug pit at a low angle for longer range. The Mk II weighed126lb, with a 46.85in barrel, and fired a 10lb HE round to minimum/maximum ranges of 275/2,750 yards. A new baseplate introduced in time for the Normandy landings enabled crews to follow advancing rifle companies more easily. See also commentary to Plate E. (Tom Laemlein/Armor Plate Press)

the Allied unit screaming for a mortar ceasefire, assuming they had received their own short rounds.

It was quickly found that 50/60mm mortar rounds had little effect on pillboxes, being too light to penetrate. The US used a light HE round in the 81mm mortar as did most other belligerents, but was the only country to also use a heavy HE round with almost three times the amount of explosive. The US M56 heavy HE was fitted with a 0.01-second delay fuze that effectively penetrated bunker roofs. Not surprisingly, US mortar units fired much more heavy HE than anticipated, and this caused faster barrel wear-out.

Mortars were also provided bursting- and/or burning-type smoke rounds for screening troop movements and blinding the enemy. White phosphorus (WP) rains burning 5,000°F (2,760°C) gobs into open-topped positions, burning through flesh and bone.

This US 75mm M1A1 pack howitzer, as issued to early-war regimental cannon companies, is hammering out direct fire over "open sights" at a close-range enemy position. Field fortifications made of earth, logs, and sandbags could seldom withstand more than a few HE rounds slammed directly into them. (Tom Laemlein/Armor Plate Press)

Attempting to wipe off the gooey burning substance only smears it on both surfaces. Immersion in water, mud, wet cloth, or petroleum jelly smothers WP, but it will re-ignite when it dries. The US, UK, and USSR used WP, but Germany did not have the capability to produce it; for burning-type projectiles all these nations also used hexachlorethane-zinc (HC). For bursting-type smoke rounds the US, UK, and Germany used titanium tetrachloride (FM); the US also used sulfur trioxide-chlorosulfonic acid (FS). These chemicals were dispersed by small bursting charges to create clouds of white smoke when exposed to air, and did not have the incendiary effects of WP. Bursting-type rounds created smoke screens more rapidly, but burning-type rounds gave a longer-lasting screen. WP, while providing the densest smoke, dissipated faster because its high temperature caused it to rise faster. Dissipating screens could be "refreshed" by firing additional rounds.

Infantry guns

The "infantry's light artillery" had much the same effects as mortars for indirect fire using HE and smoke. They were also intended for direct fire against fortifications, crew-served weapons, and personnel, and for breaching obstacles. The HE rounds could range further than most mortars and had similar effects, but they had a smaller bursting charge than mortar bombs (see panel), and smoke rounds usually generated less smoke. Most also took shaped-charge HEAT rounds, but the short barrels limited their range and accuracy; they were also slower to traverse, over more limited angles, than AT guns. They could not fire as fast as mortars, though usually faster than conventional artillery. German prisoners often said that their infantry-gun units were underemployed or contributed little to an action: this may have been true, but it might also be that the infantry-gun fire was mistaken for artillery or mortars.

Comparison of US mortar and howitzer projectiles

	81mm mortar M43A1 light HE	81mm mortar M56 heavy HE	75mm howitzer M48 HE	105mm howitzer M1 HE
Projectile weight	6.92lb	10.62lb	14.70lb	33.0lb
Bursting charge weight	1.22lb	4.3lb	1.47lb	4.8lb

Death from above: air bursts

High-explosive air-burst artillery and mortar rounds are extremely lethal and much feared. Much of an air burst's fragmentation is blasted downward, while a projectile impacting on the ground sends much of its fragmentation upward or into the ground, with considerable "blow" both forward and to the sides. Depending upon altitude, an HE projectile bursting some 20–40ft overhead could increase the fragmentation radius two or three times over that of a ground-bursting shell. Air bursts are thus particularly deadly to troops in the open and those sheltering in open-topped foxholes, trenches, and weapon pits, who are normally safe from ground-bursting shells other than the rare direct hit or impact within a couple of feet of the edge.

Soldiers under bombardment learned to keep their mouths open and hands lightly cupped over their ears, to equalize internal air pressure and help prevent eardrums from rupturing from extreme concussion, though this was in fact somewhat reduced with air bursts. Rather than hugging the bottom of a position they sat or crouched with their head just below ground level: if a near-miss cascaded earth into their position or collapsed the sides, they were near the surface rather than buried. A ground burst reflected the blast off the surface, along with rocks and other debris, causing casualties among prone troops or leg injuries to upright soldiers. Flattening on the ground, advisable when caught by a barrage in the open, only provided a bigger target for air bursts; instead, soldiers stood tight against trees, hoping for the best.

There were several ways in which rounds were caused to air-burst. Artillery HE shells could be fitted with mechanical time-delay fuzes. These had to be hand-set, with the time calculated by the fire direction center using a firing table giving the delay time for the required range. Such shell fuzes were expensive and seldom available in large numbers, and all armies lacked mechanical time fuzes for mortars. A more common method used in the European Theater was the "tree burst." Much of Europe was covered by forests and orchards, and troops dug-in within woods were highly vulnerable. Besides adding blasted-off falling branches and tree-tops to shell fragmentation, tree bursts created feet-long splinters which were hurled around like spears. Overhead cover was essential, and troops learned to cover positions with logs, limbs, scrap lumber, house doors, shutters, and mattresses. This improvised roofing was covered with flattened cardboard boxes or layers of newspaper for "waterproofing," and then with up to a foot of earth. Conventional wisdom suggested that the solution was to dig-in out in the open, but this made the positions easily detectable and permitted mortar and artillery FOs to easily deliver fire on them.

Another method of achieving air bursts was by "ricochet fire." This was accomplished by direct-fire infantry guns intentionally firing HE rounds at a low angle just short of enemy positions, so that they might ricochet up to burst overhead. However, this would not work in mud or deep snow, and anyway required a special delay fuze pre-set with a fraction of a second's delay. Such fuzes were actually intended to penetrate field fortifications, and most armies lacked them for AT and infantry guns.

The Germans possessed limited qualities of a unique air-bursting mortar round, the 8cm *Wurfgranate 39* (roughly, "bouncing projectile"). This required neither time-delay calculation nor a manual setting. It was fired in the normal manner, but upon impact a small powder charge sheared off the nose cap and blew the projectile back into the air. A fraction-of-a-second delay fuze detonated the bomb 5–10ft (or 15–20ft, depending upon which

technical reference you consult) above the ground. This munition was expensive, and was little seen in combat.

Antitank guns

Knocking out tanks required a high-velocity round, and accuracy was necessary not only to hit moving tanks at long ranges but, ideally, to place the shot on specific vulnerable points. Of course, this was almost impossible when a target tank was on the move over even level ground. The smaller-caliber AP rounds were usually solid shot, and it was found that these projectiles often glanced off the target or shattered on impact. The AP "capped" round had a blunt, softer-metal nose cap over the penetrator: upon impact, this deformed to reduce ricocheting, and dispersed the impact shock to prevent the shot from shattering. Most AP rounds had tracers to aid fire adjustment. Larger-caliber AP rounds (57mm and up) often incorporated, for behind-armor effect, a small bursting change with a base-detonating fuze, which exploded as the penetrator entered the AFV.

Most AT guns were also provided HE rounds for use against pillboxes, buildings, and troops, but these were only marginally effective owing to the small bursting change and limited fragmentation. The Russians selected 45mm caliber for their more effective HE round when most countries adopted 37mm.

Antitank rifles

The problem with AT rifles, besides their weight and bulk, was the limited penetration and even more limited behind-the-armor effect of their relatively

small bullets. The German 7.92mm round was backed by a huge propellant cartridge, but had little effect if it penetrated the armor: the small bullet ricocheting about a tank's interior had little destructive effect other than striking a crewman or two. (Some German 7.92mm AP rounds actually included a tear-gas pellet, but this had such little effect that it was not discovered until British ordnance experts dissected captured ammunition.) The British .55in and Soviet 14.5mm rounds were more effective, especially the latter, as its standard round was AP-incendiary backed by a propellant cartridge larger than some 20mm rounds. The 2cm Solothurn S-18/100 *Tankbüchse* saw limited use by Germany, Bulgaria, Italy, and the Netherlands, but despite its large caliber it used only a solid AP round.

Antitank rocket launchers

Light infantry AT guns and AT rifles were eventually supplanted in the mid-war years by man-portable, shoulder-fired rocket launchers and recoilless weapons – bazooka, PIAT, *Panzerschreck*, and *Panzerfaust*. (The Red Army did not field such a weapon until after the war, but received limited numbers of bazookas from the US.) Portable, simple, and inexpensive, these weapons gave infantrymen the ability to stalk AFVs by stealth and judicious use of concealment, reaching positions from which to attack their more vulnerable rear and flanks. Rocket launchers had their faults, however: they were relatively short-ranged, somewhat inaccurate at their maximum ranges, and caused a significant firing signature with the flash, smoke, and dust of the back-blast (which also made them dangerous to the unwary user who forgot to leave sufficient clearance space behind him, especially when within a building or fortification). Still, a man-portable weapon could now do what a truck-drawn AT gun could not.

Such weapons relied on the delivery of large-caliber high-explosive antitank (HEAT) shaped-charge projectiles capable of considerable armor penetration – typically, up to 4 or 5 inches. A limitation was that it was necessary for the rounds to strike the armor at an angle no more than 30

The bazooka-man at left is armed with a 2.36in M1A1 AT rocket launcher, and the GI at right with the M9A1. The M9 and M9A1 were fielded in early 1944– see also Plate H. Their longer tube increased the range, and the improved electrical firing system doubled the rate of fire to 10rpm. Some units retained a few M1A1s even after being issued M9s – the rockets were interchangeable. (Tom Laemlein/Armor Plate Press)

degrees from the perpendicular. At a higher angle the projectiles often glanced off without detonating, and the increasing used of sloped tank armor greatly increased the chances of deflection. (Few soldiers understood this, thinking that projectiles were deflected by thick armor.) When a shaped-charge round did penetrate the armor it created a very small hole, but shot a jet blast through it along with a molten slug, the lining of the cone-shaped warhead cavity, and fragments. It caused a blast overpressure within the AFV; while this was seldom deadly, if the molten slug and jet blast struck stowed ammunition it detonated, with catastrophic consequences.

FIRE SUPPORT UNITS

The assignment of infantry fire support weapons for each army is described here from the lowest to highest echelon within regiments.

Fire support units were subdivided into subunits of one to four weapons. Such subunits, for example a section of two MGs, were intended to operate together to support a specified infantry unit echelon. The reason for organizing them into sections or platoons of two or three weapons was that together they covered an assigned sector of fire or target area, to ensure continuous fire in event one was out of action or repositioning. In some instances there might be two sections of a certain weapon; one section would be attached to each of the two forward rifle companies, and the reserve company would not be so supported. In the event there were three sections, one could be attached to each rifle company, but this was not always so. Two might be attached to the main assault company and one to the supporting company, or the two forward companies each received a section and the third section remained under battalion control.

The various fire support subunits could be detailed out in any manner, depending on the mission, enemy opposition and tactics, terrain, fields of fire, visibility, vegetation density, and weather. A common mistake is to assume that supporting weapons should be allotted equally to all three maneuver units, e.g. line companies or battalions. It was often necessary to "weight" or more heavily reinforce certain line units depending on the above factors. In some instances it might be desirable to more heavily reinforce a regiment's reserve battalion than the lead assault battalion: the latter might have to penetrate the enemy's main line of resistance (MLR), but the reserve battalion would be committed immediately after the penetration, having to continue the assault through the depth of the enemy defenses, seize an objective, and fight off a counterattack at any stage.

Neither were support-weapon subunits necessarily detailed to line units in the defense on an equal basis. The predominance of AT weapons might be detailed to the company area through which a road or other avenue of approach ran, while the other forward company might face dense forest through which only infantry could attack. The allocation of crew-served weapons also allowed a unit to cover a wider frontage. They also increased the depth of defense when placed further to the rear, from where they might cover the forward positions and the avenues of advance through the unit's position. Fire support weapons might also be positioned to protect exposed flanks and cover gaps between units. Besides forward or in-depth defensive positions, some might be allotted to a covering force or to combat outposts forward of the MLR; here they could disorganize and weaken the advancing enemy, forcing them to deploy early into slower-moving dispersed formations. Such deployments also misled the enemy as to the location of the MLR.

Fire support subunit nomenclature

The terminology used by the different armies differed greatly. Fire support companies usually had three or four platoons, but weapons crews went by a variety of names depending on the army and type of weapon.

In the United States Army most crew-served weapons were manned by "squads," and a machine gun, mortar, or AT gun crew equaled a squad. BAR and bazooka crews were called "teams," e.g. "B-A-R team." Within regimental cannon companies, each howitzer crew constituted a "section," with two one-gun sections to a platoon. (This followed the field artillery practice of a section "crew" manning a gun, but the artillery did not have a platoon organization within the battery, simply four "gun sections.") Most infantry crew-served weapon squads were further organized into "sections" consisting of two or three one-weapon squads led by a lone NCO section leader, typically with two or three sections per platoon.

The British and Commonwealth armies called their weapons crews "detachments," usually with two detachments to a "section" and three sections per platoon for MMGs, mortars, and AT guns. Within the infantry platoon, Bren LMG, AT rifle, PIAT, and 2in mortar two- or three-man crews were called "groups," e.g. the "Bren group" of a gunner ("No. 1") and assistant gunner ("No. 2") led by a lance-corporal who was the deputy section commander.

D | **US HEAVY MACHINE-GUN SECTION, 1945**

This depicts part of a section from 29th Division in Germany, February 1945 (the two squad leaders and three of each squad's four ammunition bearers are omitted).

In the three-battalion infantry regiment, Companies D, H, and M were the battalions' heavy weapons companies, each with 1st and 2nd MG platoons (each with four .30cal M1917A1 water-cooled HMGs) and a 3rd mortar platoon (six 81mm tubes). The 36-man MG platoons were divided into a six-man HQ and two 15-man sections. Each section, led by a sergeant (staff sergeant from February 1944) comprised two seven-man squads (gun crews) each led by a corporal. There was a ¼-ton truck (jeep) in platoon HQ, which had two bazookas for self-defense, and a jeep and trailer in each squad to haul its gun, ammo, and equipment. The M1917A1 weighed 33lb, and its tripod 51lb. The squad's jeep could also be fitted with an M48 dashboard mount for the gun, but this was often omitted. For dismounted movement the squad was provided five plywood packboards: one for the gun, one for the tripod, and the others for 9x 250-rd ammo cans and the 2gal water chest.

The squad consisted of a corporal leader (sergeant, from February 1944), machine-gunner, assistant machine-gunner, and four ammunition bearers, one of whom drove the jeep. The section and squad leaders were armed with .30cal M1 rifles, the latter with an M7 grenade launcher. The gunners and assistant gunners carried .45cal pistols, and the ammunition bearers .30cal M1 carbines; the driver also had an M8 grenade launcher.

(1) Staff sergeant section leader
(2 and 3) Gunner and assistant gunner
(4) Ammunition bearer

When a two-gun section or four-gun platoon (depending upon the desired size of the "beaten zone") engaged long-range area targets by indirect fire in unison they were referred to as being "in battery." The interval between guns was 10–20 yards, to avoid both being neutralized by the same enemy fire. This section are setting up for long-range indirect fire out to 3,000 yards-plus, though accuracy was questionable beyond. 2,000 yards; sandbags stabilize the tripods. Ball or AP ammunition was used, with every fifth round a tracer. It was found that AP improved penetration through typical cover materials as well as light armor plate. The platoon HQ had a map template, drawing board, magnifying stereoscope, compasses, and binoculars to aid in identifying targets and plotting fires. Each squad had an M1917 clinometer (held here by the staff sergeant) for setting the guns' elevation for indirect fire. Besides range and angle of elevation, for long-range fire any difference in altitude between the gun and the target had to be considered; for instance, if the gun were on even a slightly higher contour than the target the "plunging fire" would fall beyond it.

In the background is an M4A1 machine-gun handcart, from which the HMG could actually be fired. Pulled by two men, it also accommodated five ammunition cans, the water chest, and a spare parts bag. A second cart carried 10 or more ammo cans, tools, and accessories. These special-issue carts were particularly useful for hauling guns and ammo from landing craft across the beach..

The Soviet equivalent to a squad was an *otdyelenie* (section), and a platoon was a *vzvod*. The MG, mortar, or AT gun crew was designated as a *rasschet* (crew), but in practice was simply referred to by the term for their weapon, e.g. "mortar" was inclusive of the crew. There were two each AT or infantry guns or three or four MGs or mortars to a platoon. There was no intermediate pairing of crew-served weapons equivalent to the US and British "section."

German HMG platoons (*schwere Maschinengewehr-Zügen*) were organized into four gun crews (*Geschütz*). These often operated in pairs called a half-platoon (*Halbzug*), or sometimes a *Staffel* (literally "echelon"), both being equivalent to a US/UK "section." Mortar platoons had three squads (*Granatwerfer-Gruppen*), each with two mortars; the crews were referred to as mortar "troops" (*Granatwerfer-Truppen*), *Trupp* here equating to a "team." AT guns and infantry guns, inclusive of the crews, were simply called a *Kanone* (cannon) or *Geschütz* (gun), respectively. A weapon crew was also referred to as a *Mannschaft* – a term with roots in ships' crews and athletic teams. A company or platoon HQ was termed a troop (*Kompanietrupp* or *Zugtrupp*). The LMG crew within a rifle squad, a platoon light mortar or AT rifle crew was also called a troop, e.g. *leichtes Maschinengewehr-Trupp* (*l MG Tr*). An exception was the late-war tank destroyer troop (*Panzer-Zerstörer-Trupp – PzZerstTr*), with three two-man *Panzerschreck* crews (*Schützen für Panzerschreck*).

Organization – squad to regiment: US Army

Fire support units and weapons allocation were based on the German example, although the capabilities of the weapons differed. Each rifle squad possessed a .30cal M1918A2 Browning Automatic Rifle (BAR), and one to three M7 rifle-grenade launchers; some squads obtained a second BAR.

The 2.36in "bazooka" AT rocket launcher began to be issued in late 1942, but many units did not receive them until mid-1943. Three were assigned to the company's weapons platoon HQ, without dedicated crews, and were detailed out to rifle platoons as needed. In February 1944 they were withdrawn from the weapons platoon, and five were assigned to the rifle company HQ; they were manned by trained squad riflemen. The battalion HQ company possessed an ammunition and pioneer platoon, and some formed bazooka teams, or .50cal MG teams using guns dismounted from unit trucks.

The rifle company's weapons platoon possessed a two-squad LMG section with 2x Browning .30cal air-cooled M1919A4 tripod-mounted guns. In late 1944 some units received the M1919A6, which could be shoulder-, bipod-, or tripod-fired. The weapons platoon's mortar section had 3x 60mm M2 tubes, which normally operated under company control. Individual mortar squads were rarely attached to rifle platoons, though they might be if conducting a patrol

Supporting the Roer river crossing in February 1945, a 4.2in (107mm) M2 heavy mortar of a US Army chemical mortar battalion fires white phosphorus rounds, quickly developing a smoke screen to blind the defenders as the assault boats cross. The "four-deuce" could fire five rounds a minute for 20 minutes, and then one round per minute indefinitely – a rate of fire that allowed it to effectively supplement field artillery. Note the ammunition: HE rounds were olive drab and WP light gray, both with yellow markings. The mortar weighed 330lb and had a 40.1in barrel; its HE round weighed 24lb 8oz, and minimum/maximum ranges were 600/4,400 yards. For comparison, the figures for the British 4.2in Mk III were 1,320lb; 61.6in; 20lb; and 1,050/4,100 yards. The Red Army also produced the 107mm PBHM-38, used by mountain troops instead of the 120mm. (Tom Laemlein/Armor Plate Press)

A US infantry battalion had six .50cal M2 Browning air-cooled heavy machine guns, and there were more at regimental level. These were intended mainly for AA use – as here in Germany, 1945 – with the M1 antiaircraft adapter fitted to an M3 tripod. All the guns were provided with these ground tripods, and were sometimes manned by HQ company volunteers in provisional MG sections. to support the rifle companies. The .50cal round could penetrate many cover materials that defeated .30cal machine guns, and maximum effective range was 2,000 yards. Frontline mobility was problematic, however: the gun weighed 84lb, the tripod another 44lb, and each 105-rd "tombstone" ammunition can 35lb. (Tom Laemlein/Armor Plate Press)

or out-posted forward of the MLR. In the defense the mortar section would plan two or three concentrations on avenues of approach, but if defending a broad frontage a 60mm might be attached to each platoon.

The infantry battalion's heavy weapons company (the regiment's Cos D, H, M, respectively) possessed two HMG platoons, each with 4x Browning .30cal water-cooled M1917A1 guns, two in each of the two sections. A full platoon or a two-gun section might be attached to each forward rifle company, with one platoon under battalion control for general support. The assault company might be supported by a full platoon, with the second platoon in general support. Alternatively one second-platoon section could be attached to the reserve company and another section kept under battalion control. If the terrain prevented the HMGs operating forward they might be positioned to the rear to provide overhead supporting fire, and/or positioned to protect flanks and cover gaps.

The heavy weapons company's mortar platoon had three sections, each with 2x 81mm M1 tubes. Sections could be attached in direct support to rifle companies, but this was usually unnecessary as the company had its own three 60mm platoon mortars. The "81s" could be more effectively employed massed under centralized control, and a battalion's frontage was seldom so wide that they could not cover the sector. Each HMG and 81mm was provided a ¼-ton truck ("jeep") and trailer.

Another battalion fire support element was the AT platoon within the HQ company. This originally had 4x 37mm M3A1 AT guns, but in mid-1943 they were replaced with 3x 57mm M1 guns. The reason the AT platoon was in the HQ company rather than the weapons company was the exaggerated early-war fear of Panzers: it was felt that placing the AT platoon under the battalion CO emphasized the importance of AT defense.

The weapons company habitually operated with all its elements attached to rifle companies or under battalion control. The company CO advised the battalion CO on heavy-weapons employment; some novice battalion COs attempted to deploy the weapons company as an entity, but this greatly

The British 2in (51mm) mortar, fired by a simple trip-lever, gave rifle platoons the ability to launch HE, smoke, and illumination rounds far beyond the range of rifle grenades. Here it is being used in the Netherlands, October 1944, by a crew from 3rd Bn Monmouthshire Regt, 11th Armoured Division. The late-war Mk VII** weighed 10lb 4oz, had a 21in barrel with a reduced-size baseplate, and could throw a 2lb 4oz HE bomb to minimum/maximum ranges of 50/500 yards. The HE round was not much more powerful than a hand grenade, however, and the mortar was most valuable for smoke-screening and illumination. The later marks lacked the earlier rectangular baseplate, carrying handle and collimator sight; they were carried slung, and aimed by eye along a white line painted on the barrel. (IWM BU1233)

restricted the weapons' capabilities and weakened the rifle companies.

The regimental cannon company was an oddity. Introduced in April 1942, it was originally equipped with 6x 75mm M1A1 pack howitzers; however, many regiments did not activate cannon companies until mid-1943 or later. In March 1943 it was proposed to eliminate the cannon company and replace it with three separate howitzer platoons assigned to the regimental HQ company, but this would not have permitted effective collective training and centralized fire planning and coordination. From July 1943 the cannon company's "pack 75s" were replaced with 105mm M3 howitzers. This "snub-nosed 105" had a shorter barrel than the standard 105mm M2A1 howitzer and offered much less range – 8,295 yards as opposed to 12,200 yards. It was mounted on a 75mm pack howitzer carriage, and lacked a shield. The cannon company provided direct and indirect fire support to the regiment, furnishing limited artillery support when divisional artillery was unavailable (which was seldom). Often, cannon companies were placed under division artillery control.

The regimental AT company was originally armed with 4x 37mm guns, which were likewise replaced by 3x 57mm guns from mid-1943. Each crew possessed a bazooka for close defense. With an often limited Panzer threat in Italy and later in Germany, the AT company saw only limited use; sometimes

A Universal carrier of a British divisional machine-gun battalion with a .303 Vickers Mk I MMG mounted for use from the vehicle; a Mk IV tripod was also stowed aboard for dismounted use. The Vickers and tripod weighed 83lb, plus about 7lb for water. Fed by 250-rd belts, its cyclic rate was 450–550rpm, but the normal expenditure was one belt every two minutes, in 25–30-rd bursts (four seconds) at six- to eight-second intervals. In 1944 a platoon's eight carriers could deliver into the frontline its four guns plus 144 boxes of ammo – an impressive total of 36,000 rounds. (Tom Laemlein/Armor Plate Press)

this was even true in France, where Panzers were more common. The AT guns were used to reduce field fortifications and defended buildings with direct HE and AP fire, but their utility was reduced by the lack of WP ammunition. The AT company also had an AT mine platoon for laying and clearing mines. Often regimental AT companies and battalion AT platoons parked their guns and augmented the understrength infantry – for mopping up, rousting out snipers, providing rear-area security, and escorting prisoners. The 57mm guns and 105mm howitzers were towed by 1½-ton cargo trucks.

A valuable non-divisional asset that sometimes supported regiments were the chemical battalions (motorized) manned by Chemical Warfare Service troops. These originally had four companies organized into three platoons each of 4x 4.2in M1A1 (1939) or M2 (1943) chemical mortars – "four-deuces" or "goon guns;" between December 1944 and February 1945 the battalions' Company Ds were inactivated to organize additional battalions. The US Army organized 32 chemical battalions between April 1942 and September 1945 (redesignated "chemical mortar battalions" between November 1944 and April 1945), of which 21 battalions saw combat. Often a battalion was attached to a division, but in some instances a battalion was split between two divisions. Typically, one company would support a regiment. Developed to deliver chemical warfare agents and smoke, in 1942 the 4.2in mortar was approved to fire HE, and thereafter it became a valued support weapon. A company could deliver more HE and WP rounds faster than a 105mm howitzer battalion, but mortars were shorter ranged – 4,400 yards as opposed to 12,200 yards.

British, Commonwealth, and Free Polish armies

These all followed the British system. Rifle platoons possessed three sections, each with a Bren LMG. The platoon HQ had a pool of light weapons, which usually had dedicated crews, but sometimes a few men were detailed to operate whichever weapons were needed. From 1938 these included a 2in Mk II hand-held mortar; this was used primarily for smoke and illumination, while HE was secondary. Two or three rifles with grenade-discharger cups were available to rifle sections. From 1937, a Boys .55in (13.9mm) Mk I AT rifle was assigned. Obsolete by 1941, it began to be replaced by the PIAT Mk I AT rocket projector in mid-1943, though some Boys were retained for soft targets.

There was no company weapons platoon; supporting weapons were concentrated at first in the HQ company, and from May 1943 in a newly introduced battalion support company. The support company possessed a mortar platoon of three sections, each with 2x 3in (actually 3.2in/81mm) Mk II mortars transported at first in 15-cwt (¾-ton) light trucks and later in Universal carriers. Each section also possessed a Boys AT rifle for close defense. A mortar section was typically attached to three of the four rifle companies depending on mission priorities; the

A Vickers section from the British 1 Commando Bde near Wesel on the east bank of the Rhine, March 1945; note green berets and Denison camouflage smocks. The tripod legs are adjusted for fire at ground level, and note that the guns are fitted with late-war "parabellum" flash-hiders. The 250-rd ammo boxes were called "liners;" they were lightweight wooden carrying-cases tightly enclosing a thin metal can with a soldered rip-off lid. Airborne and Commando units often had to fight dispersed, so the MMGs were held not as a battalion at brigade level but within the individual units, in what Commandos termed the heavy weapons troop. (IWM)

This Finnish crew, fighting alongside the Germans during their "Continuation War" against the USSR, are manning a captured Russian 7.62mm SPM-10 Maxim gun on a Kolesnikov mount; the Germans referred to this weapon as the MG216(r). Complete with its mount it weighed 99lb 11oz, plus water; its cyclic rate was 500–600rpm, and note that Russian machine guns were belt-fed from the right, while US, British, and German guns had left-hand feed.

In 1944–45 Germany raised a hundred Fortress Machine-Gun Battalions from older and less physically fit men, most of them armed with the similar World War I vintage 7.92mm Maxim MG08 to serve in the *Westwall* (see below, chapter "Example.") Complete with its sled mount the MG08 weighed 123lb 8oz plus water, compared with the 68lb 12oz of the air-cooled MG34 in its heavy configuration. It was therefore useless for mobile operations, but its sustained fire capability made it effective when emplaced in concrete bunkers and field fortifications. (Nik Cornish at www.stavka.org.uk)

main attack company might have two mortar sections in support. The AT platoon had three sections each with 2x 6-pdr Mk II AT guns towed by tracked Loyd carriers; each section also had a Bren LMG and a 2in mortar. Prior to the introduction of the 6-pdr from late 1941 the platoon was armed with 2-pdr Mk IX AT guns introduced in 1938; it was late 1942 before the 2-pdrs were fully replaced. The support company also possessed a pioneer platoon for demolition and light construction work, plus a versatile carrier platoon with 13 full-tracked Universal ("Bren gun") carriers; their armament included 13x Brens, 4x 2in mortars, and 4x PIATs.

Infantry battalion machine-gun support was provided by elements from the division's MG battalion. The three MG companies each had three four-gun platoons. A company was attached to each brigade, with a platoon going to each infantry battalion. The MMG platoon had two two-gun sections, with two Universal carriers in the platoon HQ (which also had a PIAT), one in each section HQ, and one for each gun, giving the platoon eight carriers. The guns could be ground-fired or mounted on the carrier for mobile operations. Again, prior to 1944 light trucks were used, but the section HQ had no trucks and a Boys instead of a PIAT. A particular MMG platoon might remain with the same infantry battalion for extended periods.

Additionally, from mid-1943 the MG battalion possessed a four-platoon mortar company, each platoon with 4x truck-transported 4.2in Mk III mortars; as in the US Army, these had previously equipped Royal Engineers chemical warfare units. Typically a platoon was attached to each brigade, with the fourth reinforcing the main attack or in general support. The mortars could rapidly deliver high concentrations of HE and smoke, but it was often reported that they were underutilized in 1944–45 owing to the abundance of field artillery.

The division AT regiment had four batteries each of three four-gun troops, giving 12 guns per battery. The mix of gun calibers varied over time and between divisions. Most batteries had two troops of 6-pdrs and one troop of 17-pdrs. From early 1944, AT regiments might have four batteries each with 8x 6-pdrs and 4x 17-pdrs, or two batteries with 12x 6-pdrs and two with 12x M10 SP tank destroyers, or four batteries each with 8x 6-pdrs and 4x M10s. Most eventually converted to four batteries each with 8x 17-pdrs and 4x 6-pdrs. Canadian infantry division AT regiments had 18 each towed 17-pdrs and self-propelled 17-pdr Achilles guns (M10s refitted with 17-pdrs), with three troops of six guns per battery.

The massive 17-pdr Mk I AT gun, very difficult to manhandle and conceal, was introduced in early 1943. The US-made M10 tank destroyer mounted a turreted 3in gun (almost as potent as the 17-pdr) on a modified M4 Sherman chassis. Most of these served in armored division AT regiments, but some were assigned to infantry divisions.

German Army

The early-war *Infanterie-Regiment* was similar to the US equivalent but with noteworthy differences. Rifle platoons had three rifle groups (squads), each with a 7.92mm MG34 LMG and usually a rifle-grenade launcher. Some platoons had four groups. Some companies, usually those with four-group platoons, had an HMG section of two crews with tripod-mounted MG34s, but the fourth rifle groups and HMG sections were soon dissolved as the army was expanded. Rifle platoons possessed a 5cm lGrW36 light mortar troop (crew). The company also possessed an AT rifle section with 3x 7.92mm PzB39 (*Panzerbüchse*). One might be attached to each platoon, or the section might operate together for concentrated fire. From late 1943 the Germans fielded the *Panzerfaust* single-shot AT projector, with priority to the Eastern Front, and by mid-1944 these were in widespread use on all fronts. On paper a rifle company was authorized 36, with smaller numbers to other types of companies/batteries.

Battalion MG companies (the regiment's 4th, 8th and 12th, respectively) each had three HMG platoons organized into two sections of 2x MG34s. Typically, one platoon would be attached to each rifle company, or two to the main assault company and one in general support. There was also a mortar platoon with 6x 8cm sGrW34 mortars in three two-tube squads. The platoon might be under battalion control, or one two-tube squad might be attached to each rifle company. MG companies were nicknamed *Muttergotteskinder* ("Mother of God's children"), as they were under the battalion CO's control.

The regimental infantry-gun company (13th) was organized into three platoons each with 2x 7.5cm lIG18 infantry guns and a fourth platoon with two 15cm sIG33 heavy guns – *große Spritze* ("large syringe"). Two 7.5cm platoons might support the main assault company along with the 15cm platoon, or that platoon might be in general support. Employed for both direct and indirect fire, they were to provide the regiment with immediate fire support, but were much less capable than conventional artillery.

The regimental AT company (14th) had three platoons each with 4x 3.7cm PaK35/36 AT guns towed by light trucks (the gun was nicknamed the *Türklopfer* or "doorknocker" owing to its light punch). A platoon might be attached to

The diminutive German 5cm lGrW36 light mortar was assigned one per platoon; operated by two men, it could fire six rounds in eight seconds for short periods. One crewman carried the 30lb 7oz mortar by means of this tubular steel frame harness (*Traggestell 39*), and the other ammunition in 10-rd steel cases; HE rounds weighed just under 2lb. With an 18.3in barrel, minimum/maximum ranges were 55/568 yards. Being expensive, complex, quite heavy, and of limited range and potency, it was withdrawn in 1942/43 and was not replaced at platoon level.

An early-war 8cm (actually, 81mm) German sGrW34 mortar; this weighed 125lb, had a 45in barrel, and fired a 7lb 11oz HE round to between 66 and 2,625 yards. (Comparative figures for the Red Army's standard medium mortar, the 82mm BM-37, were 126lb; 52in; 7lb 8oz; and 100/3,390 yards.) From 1942 a short-barreled 8cm kzGrW42 version was introduced, nicknamed the "*Stummelwerfer*." Weighing only 58lb 6oz with a 29.4in barrel, its minimum/maximum ranges were reduced to 55/1,203 yards. (Nik Cornish at www.stavka.org.uk)

With a weight of 880lb and a barrel length of 34.8in, the German 7.5cm lIG18 was the lightest and smallest of any Western infantry gun, but it threw a relatively heavy 12lb 11oz HE round out to 3,870 yards at a rate of 8–12rpm. It was capable of both direct and indirect fire, so its performance overlapped with that of the 8cm mortar, and from 1943 infantry-gun units were augmented with 12cm mortars. Many guns had wooden-spoke wheels (see Plate F), but those operated by this two-gun Waffen-SS *Züg* (platoon) have pneumatic tires for high-speed towing by light trucks. (Tom Laemlein/Armor Plate Press)

each battalion, or they might be allocated to cover the main avenues of tank approach. Usually two or three of a platoon's guns might be forward and the others to the rear to provide depth to the defense. Some guns might be positioned forward of the MLR. and/or to protect an exposed flank.

BRITISH 3in MORTAR DETACHMENT, 1943

The Brandt-type 3in Mk II mortar was standard for British and Commonwealth armies. Before the war the mortar platoon in the infantry battalion's HQ Company had only two tubes, and was led in 1938–40 by a warrant officer class III (the "platoon sergeant-major," an experimental rank for an NCO selected to lead a platoon in place of a commissioned officer). Early in the war some units received four mortars; by 1941 there were six, in a 46-man platoon now commanded by a second lieutenant in a four-man platoon HQ. From May 1943 the platoon was transferred to the battalion's new Support Company.

At the beginning of the war the 3in Mk II mortar had a range of only 1,600 yards, shorter than its German and Italian counterparts of the same caliber, so Axis mortarmen learned to position their weapons beyond the range of Commonwealth mortars. In North Africa, Eighth Army troops sometimes used captured mortars and ammunition for the benefit of their longer range, but the later 3in Mk V could accept enemy rounds. In the meantime the range of the Mk II was increased to 2,750 yards by using incremental propellant changes.

A mortar detachment (crew) consisted of seven men: commander (sergeant), corporal, orderly (runner), and four others. The detachment was transported in a 15-cwt truck or a tracked Universal carrier fitted with a mortar transport rack; one man was additionally designated as the driver. The platoon of three detachments was also armed with three .55in Boys AT rifles for self-defense, with a 10-magazine carrier; these were later replaced with PIATs. For effective operation each mortar required a crew of four. When dismounted from their vehicle, No. 1 (sergeant commander) carried the baseplate and sight, No. 2 (corporal) the barrel and spare parts bag, No. 3 the adjustable bipod, and No. 4 ammunition, in 3-rd fiberboard carrier tubes secured with two metal bands and wooden wedges.

During firing, the No.1 was on the mortar's left, laying the barrel and giving firing commands; No. 2 acted as loader, on the right; No. 3 readied the rounds – checking the external

"augmenting cartridges," unscrewing the nose safety cap, and passing bombs to the loader; and No. 4 opened the carrier tubes, which were closed by tin lids each end held on by narrow. snap-fastened fabric handle-straps around the whole carrier. In the frontline the actual ranks of the No. 1 and No. 2 were often more junior than prescribed by regulations, due to slow replacement of NCO casualties. The No. 1 depicted here (badged as serving with 5th Bn Hampshire Regt, 128 Inf Bde, 46th Inf Div in Italy, October 1943) is a corporal, and the rest of the crew are privates.

The carrier tubes were roughly painted with a yellow band for HE and a green band for WP smoke rounds. The 10lb HE bombs were filled with 1.2lb of 80/20 Amatol topped with TNT, and detonated by a No. 162 direct-action fuze; a No. 390 delay fuze was used for smoke and illumination ("star") rounds. HE rounds were painted with a "copal" varnish giving a bronze-brown finish, with a red filling band high on the shoulder; the tail tube (factory-filled with a ballistite propellant charge) and vanes were black; augmenting cartridges were originally celluloid, but by mid-war were cylindrical fabric bags of a greasy buff color, attached between the vanes by metal bands through the vane holes. A detachment had an initial allotment of 120 rounds.

All armies specified circular or square dug-in mortar positions (in Commonwealth armies, 6ft x 10ft x 3½ft deep), but crews seldom had time to dig in properly and often used natural depressions, shallow scraped pits, or any available natural cover – craters, ditches, walls, or rubble. Note in the back of this pit (left to right): one of the crew's SMLE rifles; a spare black-and-white aiming post, as set up for use as a reference point for fire adjustment (most armies used red-and-white posts); a Boys AT rifle and magazine-carrier; a mortar cleaning rod; a T-handle shovel; and a machete for clearing brush. The No. 1 has the leather sight case slung, and holds the muzzle cover; long use has burned paint off the barrel.

The German 15cm sIG33 heavy infantry gun was the largest of this category used by any army – at 3,859lb and with a 64.9in barrel, it was as big as a field artillery pierce. A two-gun platoon served beside three 7.5cm platoons within the regimental infantry-gun company. Its range of 5,140 yards was much shorter than that of most artillery pieces, but its 84lb shell was capable of destroying field fortifications, breaching obstacles, and blasting buildings and troop concentrations. It could be towed with a limber by a team of six horses, a medium truck, or a light halftrack. (Courtesy Concord Publications)

The foregoing was the core organization and equipment. As the army expanded new weapons were fielded, shortages in some weapon categories occurred, and tactics were changed, so many units were differently organized and armed.

During the immediate early-war expansion many new regiments lacked 8cm mortars until production caught up, and might have only four light infantry guns. Other regiments lacked any infantry guns, but the 13th Co was armed with 8x 8cm mortars in two platoons. In the spring of 1940 new regiments had no infantry-gun or AT companies, but a single 13th heavy (*schwere*) company with a mix of four light infantry guns and four AT guns. In late 1940, most new regiments had no mortars or infantry guns and only a single AT platoon. Regiments raised in 1941 and 1942 might not receive their 13th and 14th Cos until 1944/45. In 1942/43 the 5cm mortars were withdrawn, being judged too heavy, costly, and impotent to be worth the trouble, and were partly replaced by the 8cm kzGrW42 short-barreled mortar known as the *Stummelwerfer* ("stump projector"). In 1941 the 5cm PaK38 began replacing the 3.7cm AT gun, but due to shortages the 3.7cm remained in use long afterwards.

In October 1943, the New Type (*neuer Art*) infantry division was introduced. Regiments lost their III Battalion, but the previous 13th and 14th regimental companies retained those designations. Remaining battalions were reorganized with three rifle companies, each with 16x MG34/42 and a section of 2x 8cm kzGrW42 mortars. The battalion MG companies (4th and 8th) each had 12x HMGs, 3x LMGs, and 4x 12cm sGw43 heavy mortars. The infantry-gun company (13th) had 6x 7.5cm and 2x 15cm, plus 5x LMGs. The AT company (14th) was to have 12x 7.5cm PaK40 or 7.62cm Pak36(r) AT guns; the latter was a widely used German AT modification of the Russian FS-22 field gun, some being rechambered for German 7.5cm ammunition. Many companies had mixes of 5cm and 7.5/7.62cm guns. The three-company divisional AT battalions might have 4x 3.7cm and 6x 5cm in each mixed company, but more often had different mixes including some 7.5/7.62cm guns. Elements of these battalions could be attached to infantry regiments and battalions.

Another organizational revision occurred in late 1944 with the new Type 44 *Volksgrenadier-Division*. The infantry battalion now had a heavy

company rather than an MG company; this possessed a platoon of 4x 7.5cm infantry guns, two HMG platoons with 4x MG34/42 apiece, and a platoon with 6x 8cm mortars. The infantry-gun company (13th) had 4x light or 2x light and 2x heavy infantry guns, and 8x 12cm mortars in two platoons. The AT company (14th) was now called the tank destroyer company (*Panzer-Zerstörer*). This was organized into three platoons of three squads, each squad having two six-man "troops" with 3x 8.8cm RPzB54 *Panzerschrecken*, giving the company up to 54 rocket launchers plus 18 spares.

The final reorganization was the *Infanterie-Division 45*. The new battalion heavy companies did not have HMGs, but a platoon of 4x light infantry guns and a platoon of 6x 8cm mortars. The regimental heavy company (13th) had 2x 15cm infantry guns and 8x 12cm mortars – referred to as the *Heeresfeuerwehr* ("army fire protection" or fire department), as they were employed to face enemy attacks and breakthroughs. The tank destroyer company (14th) was the same as in the *Volksgrenadier-Division*.

Soviet Red Army

The Russians had more fire support elements organic to the rifle regiment than any other belligerent. However, being perpetually engaged, suffering massive troop and equipment losses, and relying on very variable production and distribution capabilities, it was seldom that regiments had anywhere near the authorized allocation.

The rifle regiment's three battalions each had three rifle companies, with three rifle platoons and a mortar platoon. Rifle platoons had four sections, two with one 7.62mm Degtaryev DP or DPM LMG and the other two with two guns; often there were fewer LMGs. The mortar platoon had 2x 50mm RM-39, -40, or -41 mortars, and an MG section with a single 7.62mm Maxim SPM-10 HMG on a hand-drawn wheeled mount.

Battalions had two each fire support companies and platoons. The MG company had three platoons with a total of 9x SPM-10 HMGs. The mortar company had three platoons each with 3x 82mm RM-36, -37, or -41 tubes. The AT gun platoon had 2x 45mm M1937 or M1942 guns. Owing to a shortage of guns the battalion AT platoons were dropped in July 1941, but restored in January 1943. Finally, the AT rifle platoon had 3x 14.5mm Degtyarov PTRD-41 or Simonov PTRS-41 rifles.

Infantry regiments likewise had four fire support companies and batteries. The AT gun battery fielded 6x 45mm guns; the infantry-gun battery had 4x 76mm M1927/37 guns; the mortar battery had 6x 120mm HM-38 or -43 tubes; and the AT rifle company had 27 rifles in three platoons of nine.

Attached field artillery

Apart from their organic support elements, in all armies infantry regiments typically had a light artillery battalion in direct support. If attacking, it might be supported by additional battalions including medium artillery. The artillery battalion operating in direct support of a regiment was seldom under its control; more commonly it remained under division control so that it could switch support to other units when necessary. The equipment of light artillery battalions supporting regiments/brigades were as follows (note that British artillery "regiments" were structured as battalions):

US Field Artillery Battalion: 3x four-gun batteries (105mm M2A1 howitzer)

UK Field Regiment, Royal Artillery: 3x eight-gun batteries (25-pdr/87mm Mk II gun-howitzer)

USSR Artillery Battalion: 3x four-gun batteries (76mm ZiS-3 field gun)

German Artillery Battalion: 3x four-gun batteries (10.5cm lFH18 light field howitzer)

(The German 8.8cm Flak gun was *not* standard to divisional field artillery, despite virtually every memoir claiming to recall being shelled by "eighty-eights." While employed as ad hoc AT guns they were little used in the field artillery role, being ill-suited for indirect fire.)

The Red Army viewed infantry guns, mortars, and AT guns, regardless of how small the caliber, as being integrated with the artillery, and gave them a greater tactical role than in other armies. A rifle regiment, for example, might consolidate the regimental 120mm mortar battery (six tubes) and the three battalions' 82mm mortar companies (nine tubes each) into a "*groupment*" (essentially a provisional battalion) with 33 mortars under centralized control. The massed mortars would be assigned close-range targets, and also employed for counter-mortar fires. (This does not mean the mortars were physically massed – the companies were positioned around the regimental sector.) This groupment could lay down a considerable amount of saturating area fire at up to 3,000 yards – a 6-rd volley amounted to 198 rounds delivered within 20 seconds. Only the two company 50mm mortars directly supported rifle

Infantry regiment/brigade fire support elements, 1944

Fire support elements within regiments/brigades are noted in bold type, and the echelon at which they were integrated is shown by their relative indentation.

US Infantry Regiment	German Inf Regt	Soviet Rifle Regt	British Inf Brigade
HQ & HQ company	Staff co	Regimental HQ	Brigade HQ
Infantry battalion (x3)	Inf bn (x3)*	Rifle bn (x3)	Infantry bn (x3)
HQ & HQ company	Staff co	Bn HQ	HQ co
Rifle company (x3)	Rifle co (x3)	Rifle company (x3)	Rifle co (x4)
Rifle platoon (x3)	Rifle ptn (x3)	Rifle ptn (x3)	Rifle ptn (x3)
Weapons platoon	**AT section**	**Mortar ptn**	**Support company**
Heavy weapons company	**MG co**	**MG co**	Light aid det (attached)
Cannon company	**Inf gun co**	**Mortar co**	Ground defence ptn
AT company	**AT/tank destroyer co**	**AT rifle ptn**	**MG co (attached)**
Service company	Train	**AT gun platoon**	**Heavy mortar ptn**
Medical detachment		**SMG co**	Attached services
		AT rifle company	
		AT gun battery	
		Infantry-gun bty	
		Mortar bty	
		Regimental services	

Note:

* Most German regiments were reduced to two battalions in 1944, but retained complete regimental fire support units.

companies. The regiment might additionally be supported by an artillery groupment of one or more divisional 76mm field gun battalions, possibly augmented by a battery or more of 122mm M1910/30 howitzers, for direct-fire support to engage the enemy's forward positions, bunkers, and defended buildings, and to breach obstacles. An infantry battalion might be directly supported by a sub-groupment of these weapons, and the 76mm regimental infantry-gun battery might be attached to one of these sub-groupments.

TACTICAL EMPLOYMENT

Regardless of what doctrine was outlined in manuals and what was taught army-wide, individual units within all armies habitually developed their own methods based on their experiences, the terrain they fought on, the climate, enemy tactics, and available resources. US divisions and even regiments within the same division routinely established their own tactics. For example, in late 1944 the US 9th Inf Div established a six-step system to defeat Siegfried Line bunkers: (1) Approach as close as possible with a rifle platoon and engineer squad. (2) Employ tanks, tank destroyers, AT guns, or bazookas for supporting fire. (3) Suppress the bunker with mortars and artillery. (4) Employ direct-fire weapons to suppress embrasures and entrances. (5) Close in with infantry and engineers, using smoke. (6) Destroy the bunker using demolitions on the roof or by pointblank fire from supporting weapons. As can be seen, all types of infantry direct- and indirect-fire support weapons –

MGs, AT guns, mortars, and bazookas – were employed, along with field artillery and tank and tank-destroyer guns; even self-propelled 155mm guns might be employed as direct-fire weapons.

Fire control

Field artillery battalions employed forward observers to locate targets, and request and adjust fire. In the US they were simply called forward observers (FO), while the British termed them forward observation officers (FOO), and the Germans observation officers (*Beobachtungsoffizier*). Battery commanders sometimes doubled as FOs, as did infantry-gun company commanders. The Soviets used battery and weapons company commanders as FOs. In the US Army, three-man FO sections were assigned to divisional 105mm howitzer batteries and to the battalion, but none to other types of artillery battalions. There were also three liaison sections that coordinated fires with the infantry battalions. The 105mm battalions' FOs attached to infantry regiments and battalions handled all calls for fire, through centralized fire direction centers at division artillery and artillery group levels. (One British infantry company commander wryly recalled that his essential job had been simply to escort FOOs across Europe – a testament to the importance of supporting firepower.)

Infantry guns and mortars were seldom tied into the artillery fire control system, except in the Red Army, but American cannon companies were sometimes integrated into the division artillery, as were 4.2in mortar units. In most instances, FOs for these weapons were the weapons company CO and/or his platoon leaders. Battalion mortar platoon leaders also served as FOs. Rifle company commanders might direct supporting weapons, being linked into the battalion telephone net. FOs positioned themselves where they could observe specific target areas to support a planned assault. In the defense they took up positions where they could observe as much of the company's or battalion's sector as possible. Ideally, the FO was as close to the gun-target line as possible, which helped speed adjustments and improve accuracy; unless absolutely necessary, they would position themselves no more than 100 yards from the gun-target line.

An OP could be anything from an elaborately prepared, dug-in, and camouflaged position, to a building's second-story window, a church steeple, a shell crater that the FO jumped into, or a bush on a hillside. Conventional wisdom and the need for FOs to observe large areas dictated that OPs were placed on the highest elevation in the sector. Such positions were often too conspicuous for survivability; church towers, obvious hilltops, and lone buildings were usually avoided, since they tended to attract suppressive fire. The Germans sometimes blew down steeples when withdrawing to deny Allied FOs vantage points. While they were sometimes used for lack of any other options, more commonly "second best" positions that would attract less fire were selected: wrecked buildings, nondescript clumps of trees and brush, and knocked-out vehicles. Some FOs used telephone linesmen's climbing spurs to shimmy up trees, but trees were not always good vantage points. In a forest of roughly equally high trees a man could not climb high enough to see over the other trees, as the limbs were too small to support or conceal him. Suitable OP trees had to be in clumps with shorter trees, or on the edge of a wood line.

Camouflage was essential, and care had to be taken to avoid reflection from binoculars, telescopes, and rangefinders; German snipers searched for men using binoculars, as well as radio operators, so it was necessary to conceal radio antennas. Since OPs were ideally positioned to view the

Forward observers were essential for locating targets, determining the appropriate type of ammunition and fuzing, making fire corrections, and reporting the results. Here a *Sonderführer* war correspondent interviews a gunner on observation duty (though the actual FO would be an officer). He uses a 6x30 Sf14Z *Scherenfernrohr* (scissors binocular), also known as *Eselsohren* ("donkey's ears"); the Americans and British called this a battery commander's telescope or "BC scope." Allied equivalents were all very similar to this German model: vertical dual periscope-type telescopes which, being stereoscopic, provided more definition at longer ranges and improved range estimation. (Courtesy Concord Publications)

battlefield, there was the danger that commanders and staffs would visit and might be careless when moving about, immediately attracting fire from opposing FOs. Most OPs were close behind the frontline, but sometimes, especially during attacks, FOs infiltrated to positions beyond the frontline – what the Germans called a *vorgeschobenen Beobachtungsstelle* (*VBSt*) or advanced OP, and the Russians a *nablyudatel'nii punkt komandira polka* (*PPA*) or forward OP. In armored and mechanized units the FO might ride in the command vehicle or even have his own AFV to keep pace with the advancing column. As foot units advanced FOs could accompany them, usually with the CO. On the other hand, FOs might remain behind to provide over-watch for the assault troops if terrain, fields of observation, and visibility permitted. Fog, rain, and snow severely hampered this, but remaining behind allowed the existing telephone-wire system to be used for a time. The FOs would then move to the infantry's new position on their secured objective, but preferably not until after the enemy had counterattacked it.

Communications

Lightweight tactical radios were scarce, even for FOs, and most available radios were dedicated to the command net. The FO usually had a radio that was set with a frequency range for the artillery, which was different from the frequencies set in infantry radios. The frequency ranges overlapped, but they might have been assigned to other units and FOs were unable to use the overlapping frequencies. This made it essential for the FOs to accompany companies. The radios of the era were heavy, bulky, temperamental, short-ranged, and more affected by atmospherics than today's (see Elite 181, *World War II Battlefield Communications*), and quickly burned through their heavy batteries. US and British FOs usually had radios, which gradually improved; German FOs might or might not have radios. For most of the war the Red Army was severely short of radios and even field telephones, which often forced them to rely on rigid fire plans: FOs could not relay fire requests, corrections, or orders to lift, shift, or cease fire other than by flares. From 1944, American Lend-Lease radios and telephones improved Soviet fire control.

Radios were especially useful during mobile operations, especially when advancing rapidly, but even when they were available FOs established wire nets as a backup, and often preferred telephones for primary communications. They were more reliable and offered clearer reception than radios, and radio nets could be monitored by the enemy (not that this provided a great deal of actionable intelligence: it was extremely "perishable" in rapidly changing tactical situations, and anyway armies lacked the resources for much radio direction-finding at the tactical level). Telephone wire could be cut by shelling,

---

F | **GERMAN 7.5cm LIGHT INFANTRY-GUN PLATOON, 1940**

Known as the *Infanterie Sieben-Funf* ("infantry seven-five") or simply as *Stumpf* ("stumpy"), the *7.5cm leichte Infanterie-Geschütz 18* was a miniature artillery piece optimized for close-range fire support. It was mainly intended for attacking pillboxes and other strongpoints using direct or (as here) indirect fire, but the 8cm mortar made it somewhat redundant. Infantry guns were more complex and expensive to manufacture than mortars, and demanded more crew training. On the plus side, the *Stumpf* could lob a 12lb 11oz shell 3,870 yards – about 800 yards further than the 8cm *mGrW34* mortar. The fuze could be set for instantaneous detonation or a 0.15-second delay to penetrate overhead cover, though the heavy projectile had only a 1.44lb bursting charge similar to that of the lighter mortar bomb.

The 7.5cm used semi-fixed ammunition: i.e. the projectile was removed from the shell case, propellant increments were removed ("cut") to adjust the range, the projectile was refitted, and then the round was loaded as a complete cartridge. Three rounds were carried in wicker, wooden, or metal boxes. The gun's direct-fire capability was useful against point targets and it could also engage AFVs, but its shaped-charge round only achieved a 55mm penetration. It was less accurate than high-velocity AT guns; its handwheel traverse was slow, covering an arc of only 12 degrees; and its rate of fire was 8–12rpm, only about half that of a practiced mortar crew. At 880lb it was also heavy, and the gun and the limber for "ready" ammunition and equipment required four draft horses (though two could be used over short distances); four more were needed for each

gun's second limber and ammo caisson. The eight-gun horse-drawn *Infanteriegeschütz-Kompanie* officially had 88 draft horses and 45 riding horses, though often fewer in practice (the company's two 1.5-ton *sIG33* heavy infantry guns required six horses for the gun and limber, and a 13-man crew). Their role meant that guns had to be repositioned so often that they were nicknamed *Zigeunerartillerie* ("gypsy artillery"). While the *lIG18* could be manhandled over the shortest distances by the crew using heavy leather or canvas hooked slings (*Schleppriemen*, as worn here by the two "ammunition numbers"), its relative unwieldiness, and the great logistic burdens imposed by the need for horse-teams, compared badly with the 8cm mortar's weight of 125lb, which could be carried by three men or in a handcart.

Each infantry-gun platoon had an 11-man HQ (*Zugtrupp*), and two guns each with a 10-man crew (including two farriers for the horse-teams – which in this view are presumably sheltering behind the farmhouse). In practice four men could operate it, as depicted: an NCO gun commander, a gunner, and two ammunition handlers. If the unit was motorized the guns were fitted with rubber tires, and each gun and caisson was towed by a light field car. The gunshield was intended to protect the crew from MG fire, and the hinged apron at the bottom was raised when the gun was under tow. Note the shield's wavy edges, and the prewar brown-and-green camouflage pattern, both intended to make it less conspicuous against vegetation. Most artillery, being deployed well to the rear, was finished in the solid color considered sufficient to hide it from high-flying aircraft, but infantry and AT guns in the frontline were often camouflage-painted.

Besides forward observers, another key aspect of fire support was provided by liaison officers and NCOs from artillery and fire support units, who were detailed to the command post of the infantry unit they supported. They advised the infantry unit's command staff on the capabilities and limitations of the fire support unit; coordinated unit locations, ammunition resupply, radio frequencies, and wire nets; and integrated the fire support unit into the developing operation order. Here a US 3rd Armd Div officer undertakes coordination on an SCR-510 radio mounted on a jeep; the "510" was specifically designed for use by artillery liaison and FOs. (Tom Laemlein/Armor Plate Press)

whether suspended in trees or laid on the ground, and was most frequently cut by friendly vehicle traffic. Burying miles of wire that would have to be recovered later was totally impractical in terms of available manpower and time. In most armies, linemen laid wire "downwards" from units to subordinate subunits, but FOs were accompanied by one or two wiremen who laid wire to their own OP. Besides links to the weapons subunits they controlled, fire support CO/FOs might be connected to the CP they supported and were often on the same telephone net as battalion and company COs. This allowed COs to request and adjust fire in their sectors. In the attack, FOs advanced with the units they supported and laid wire behind them to maintain contact with the firing subunits if radios were not available (or even if they were, to ensure contact was maintained).

Messengers (US), runners (British), *peshii* (Russian), and *Melder* (German) were the most basic alternate means of communications. Messengers were not effective for relaying firing orders and corrections from FOs to the guns owing to the time-distance delay, but were used to coordinate the firing element with the unit headquarters and between gun crews. Colored flares or smoke fired from signal pistols or grenade launchers were frequently used to signal orders to commence, lift, shift, or cease fire. FOs or infantry leaders might fire these signals according to a pre-arranged schedule, or when necessary.

If possible, supporting weapons, especially indirect-fire weapons, were positioned to support not only the attack, but to be able to fire on any enemy counterattack from the same positions. This was not always possible, and sooner or later the weapons would have to be displaced forward, creating a time gap when they were unable to fire. Sometimes part of the weapons subunit – e.g. two mortars – would be moved forward, while the other four remained in readiness to move up once the first weapons were in position and registered. The telephone wire would have to be recovered, repaired, and readied for re-use in the next advance.

Planning

Mortar and infantry-gun fires were normally pre-planned. In the defense, barrages were plotted on likely infantry avenues of approach, especially in heavily overgrown and rough terrain offering cover and concealment. Obstacles and minefields had to be covered by fire, since they were easily breached. Roads and other avenues of vehicle approach would also have barrages plotted on them, not necessarily with the expectation of destroying AFVs with indirect fire, but of forcing them to "button-up" and disperse; this disorganized their formations, blinded them with smoke and dust, and separated them from their infantry. Other targets might be possible positions where the attackers would emplace their own supporting direct-fire weapons, OPs, assembly areas, attack positions, etc. Defensive fires were plotted a safe distance from the forward positions. Registration or target points were also plotted, usually on easily identifiable terrain features which could still be made out on all but the darkest nights.

Antitank troops of a German *Schützen-Regiment* hand-push a 3.7cm AT gun forward following light trucks transporting riflemen. The gun was loaded, set on "safe," and otherwise prepared to fire, so that it did not have to be unlimbered and turned around before engaging sudden targets. Crewmen carried additional rounds, and more could be brought up from the rear. (Courtesy Concord Publications)

Registration firing involved firing one mortar or gun per section, platoon, or battery. This would be the "base gun," either the left-hand or a center gun. This was to avoid alerting the enemy by firing a larger number of rounds, and to conserve ammunition. When new targets emerged that were not within preplanned barrage areas, FOs adjusted fire from the nearest registration point. An initial round would be fired in relation to a reference point (British, target number; German and Soviet, orientation point) – for example: "RP 4. Left 200. Down 50." Distances were given in yards by the Western Allies, but the US and British also quoted meters when using Continental European maps. Further adjustments would be made to bring single rounds onto the new target, or at least to "bracket" it – i.e. by one round above and one below, or rounds to both flanks. Then a final estimated visual adjustment was made that would bring the following barrage onto the target, and the support unit was ordered to "fire for effect" X-number of rounds (sometimes a number of guns less than the total was specified).

The Red Army routinely positioned heavy machine guns well forward, to place sustained suppressive fire on enemy positions to cover the infantry assault. Unlike Western armies, they seldom used HMGs for long-range indirect fire; this was due not only to tactical doctrine, but also to limited crew training and technical skills. This 7.62mm Maxim SPM-10 is mounted on an old-fashioned Sokolov two-wheeled mount with shield. The alternative Kolesnikov mount, which had a longer trail fitted with a gunner's seat, was also used with the SPM-10, and – often with the shield removed, as in the photo on page 34 – for the later replacement 7.62mm SG-43, though the SPM-10 remained in use throughout the war. (Tom Laemlein/Armor Plate Press)

Usually the FO directed the number and type of rounds, and specified fuzing. Final defensive fires would be planned just forward of the frontline positions, and even on and behind the positions in the event they were overrun and to support a counterattack by own troops. Fire might also be plotted to protect the unit's flanks in case of a breakthrough in an adjacent unit's sector.

Weapons employment

In the attack, preplanned targets would be coordinated: known enemy positions, defended buildings, suspected reserves, rear facilities (ammunition, supply points), CPs, OPs, obstacles needing breaching, etc. Registration points would be designated and logged.

AT guns were excellent for direct long-range fire, "long-range" here meaning to engage targets within visual range on battalion and regimental battlefields. For their primary mission they covered AFV avenues of approach. Some might be emplaced forward of the MLR (as described above); most were positioned in the frontline, and others in the depth of the defense. On terrain where forests, broken ground, and mud prevented AFVs maneuvering cross-country AT guns covered roads through the depth of the defense, so a force restricted to advancing on a road axis might face one AT gun after another. They were reinforced with mines, roadblocks, blown bridges and culverts, booby-trapped obstacles, and tank-hunter teams. AT guns could secure the flanks and cover gaps between units, and advancing units would "drop off" AT guns to cover roads leading into their flanks.

They were also valuable in the absence of AFVs; direct fire against point targets saw them using HE to engage bunkers, MG nests, buildings, obstacles, and troops, as well as point targets requiring accurate fire such as church steeples or specific windows occupied by FOs or snipers. Speed of employment was critical; the British, for example, required their battalion AT guns to arrive on the infantry's objective within 15 minutes of securing it, to prepare for the German counterattack expected within a half-hour, though this was impossible in heavily overgrown or broken terrain. AT guns were difficult to conceal in urban areas, and hiding them with rubble was the preferred method. In some instances AT guns were positioned and camouflaged on side streets some distance from an intersection, to fire on passing tanks from the flank.

G

SOVIET 45mm ANTITANK GUN
INFANTRY SUPPORT ROLE, 1943

This 45mm M1937 AT gun was a scaled-up version of the 37mm M1930. It weighed 1,257lb; its 3lb 2oz AP-tracer round, fired from a 66.8in barrel, could penetrate 60mm (2.36in) of armor at 500 meters and 55mm (2.16in) at 1,000 meters. This made it effective for side but not frontal shots against most German tanks. The Red Army had chosen 45mm caliber over 37mm partly because it also offered an effective HE/fragmentation shell for anti-personnel use, as well as smoke and canister rounds.

The M1937's barrel was lengthened to 116.8in for the 45mm M1942 AT gun, which also featured other upgrades to improve velocity, accuracy, and range. In its turn, the M1942 began to be replaced for AT use with the superior 57mm ZiS-2 from 1943. Since it was allocated at infantry regimental level the M1937 then became in effect a direct-fire support weapon, in which role its ammunition made it valuable for suppressive fire against troops and positions. Added to 76mm infantry guns, 82mm and 120mm mortars, and AT rifles, it gave the Red Army regiment substantial fire support. The M1937's fast firing rate of 15–20rpm made it effective in short-range ambushes, for which guns were often deployed singly, though they might also be grouped.

Here a crew have just fired a canister round at a squad of German bicycle-reconnaissance *Radfahrtruppen* on a forest track. During a prepared defense the gun could be dug in, but crews more often used any available cover and concealment; the top one-third of the shield could be folded forward to lower the profile. The 7mm gunshield, like those of most AT guns, had a hinged apron to guard against ground ricochets, and was often reinforced with sandbags.

Regimental AT batteries had a six-man battery HQ, and three two-gun, 17-man platoons; from 1943 an extra platoon was added at battalion level. Guns were towed by four horses and a caisson, or by a variety of light trucks.

Italy, 1944: a British 3in Mk II mortar mounted in a Universal carrier, from which it could fire or be dismounted for ground use. The carrier, accommodating 51 mortar rounds in the side compartments, allowed the mortar to be moved to just about any position, and over the worst terrain it could then be man- or mule-packed.

Ammunition interchangeability

Although the rounds for Brandt-type 81mm mortars were of slightly different designs, and were variously designated 8cm, 8.1cm, 8.14cm, 81mm, or 81.4mm, most were interchangeable. Exceptions were usually due to the design of mortar firing pins or of particular projectiles. The British 3in (actually 3.2in/81.3mm) Mk II mortar could not fire German and Italian bombs because of the design of the tube's base and firing pin, and remained in common use even after the introduction of the Mk V, which was redesigned to accept Axis ammunition. The Soviet 82mm models could fire German 81mm rounds, but the Germans had to fire their own ammunition from the large numbers of Russian mortars they captured. Before using foreign ammunition armies had to carry out field tests to accommodate different firing tables, barrel lengths, projectile weights, and propellant charges. Ranges varied greatly between 81mm models, but most reached 2,500 to 3,000 yards-plus. (Tom Laemlein/ Armor Plate Press)

HMGs provided direct and indirect fire, although often they were optimally positioned to undertake only one of those missions. They were typically positioned to deliver overhead fire, that is, firing over the forward friendly positions or advancing troops. This naturally had to be closely coordinated, and lines of fire between advancing units were preferred. In dense terrain with heavy vegetation and rugged ground, or in urban areas, HMGs could not always deliver overhead long-range fires, and COs might place them in the frontline to maximize firepower rather than leaving them in the rear. (It appears to have been a common mistake of some "by the book" commanders to insist that HMGs be employed strictly as doctrine specified.) The Germans routinely employed their HMGs as LMGs, attaching them to rifle companies when terrain and vegetation prevented their standard use. The commonality of their basic air-cooled weapon made this feasible: they merely dismounted the guns from their sustained-fire tripods and reinforced the assault units. HMGs could also secure the flanks and cover gaps between units.

Supporting weapons platoons, sections, and squads might be kept under the control of their parent company; kept essentially under battalion or regimental control; or attached for direct support to rifle companies. In the latter case the weapons subunit might still be following a battalion or regimental fire plan, but the rifle company CO could direct them to support his actions. They could also be placed under the direct control of rifle companies, or withdrawn and reassigned another mission at any time.

Battalion and brigade mortars were incorporated into Montgomery's typically heavy barrages in NW Europe. At the turn of 1944/45 German mortars and multi-tube *Nebelwerfers* were causing up to 70 percent of Anglo-Canadian casualties. Sound-locating was inadequate owing to the

A US 10th Mtn Div 81mm mortar section of two squads provides supporting fire from well-sandbagged, dug-in positions in northern Italy, 1945. Separate mortar sections typically provided direct support to individual rifle companies, but in the mountains – owing to narrow frontages, and limited suitable ground for firing positions – the battalion mortar platoon often operated as a single unit. The mortar section's two squads (crews) each consisted of eight men. The two-man section headquarters officially consisted of a second lieutenant and a staff sergeant, since sections were envisaged as operating separately. No other country assigned an officer to lead a two-tube section, and in practice shortages of junior officers usually prevented them from actually doing so. (Tom Laemlein/Armor Plate Press)

mortars' negligible sound and the *Nebelwerfers*' ripple fire, so a counter-mortar program was established using trailer-mounted Mk III gun-laying radars. The 1st Canadian and 100th British Radar Batteries were operational in this role in January 1945, and although accuracy fell short of today's standards they did help to reduce casualties.

From 1944 the German forward defenses featured large number of machine guns, most riflemen being dug-in further back to launch counterattacks, and the mortars some 3,000–4,000 yards back. An attacker had to break through the defense and thrust quickly to the rear to overrun the mortars. The Wehrmacht increasingly employed *Panzerfausts* and *Panzerschrecks* in depth, along with SP armored assault guns as mobile pillboxes.

It is often assumed that specific supporting weapons elements were habitually attached to the same infantry units. This was often not the case, owing to the needs to give infantry units additional fire support, to allow weapons subunits rotation for rest and maintenance, and to reinforce understrength units. Even in training, weapons subunits would rotate between the infantry units they supported to gain familiarity. Supporting weapons platoon leaders and platoon and section sergeants often served as liaison agents to coordinate fires with the infantry battalion's companies. They might also accompany battalion and company COs when new positions were reconnoitered or when the unit

This German mGrW34 mortar is set up in a pit with a blind of wire-woven wheat stalks to mask its muzzle flash and the dust raised by firing; the dust might also be wetted down. It was almost impossible to hide the flash at night, but darkness made it more difficult for enemy FOs to estimate the range. More often than not mortars were set up in or behind any available cover, which also hampered enemy efforts to locate them by sound-ranging (which was usually impossible anyway, owing to their minimal noise). Adequate cover became even more essential late in the war, when the Western Allies began using the first crude counter-mortar radar techniques. (Tom Laemlein/Armor Plate Press)

A Russian 45mm M1937 AT gun still bearing its winter paint scheme; an "ammunition number" lying in the right background holds a ready-round taken from a four-shell crate. Unusually, this photo includes the two-horse ammunition limber, positioned to allow the gun to be quickly hitched up and moved to a new position. (Tom Laemlein/Armor Plate Press)

relieved another in the line. An essential part of supporting weapons employment was the reconnaissance, selection, and occupation of positions. Leaders would select firing positions and the routes to them, and identify ammunition points and prime-mover parks (whether for trucks or draft horses). If relieving a unit, the existing firing positions were occupied and the in-place unit turned over target reference points, barrage areas, and other firing data (and in the closest terrain would even swap their weapons). Enemy positions would be pointed out, and the relieving unit would be briefed on recent activity. The relieved unit also often left most of their ammunition and their field telephone wire net.

Supporting weapons required significant space within a unit's sector. For instance, a German three-battalion infantry regiment, with two battalions deployed on the MLR and one in reserve, had nine rifle companies on the ground, plus battalion and regimental CPs, supply and ammunition points, aid stations, over a dozen baggage and supply trains, attached engineers, and more. To these were added the supporting weapons subunits: four infantry-gun platoons, three of AT guns, three of mortars, and nine of HMGs – 19 fire support platoons. Since most of these subunits were in the frontline or close behind, their dispersal had to be considered with a view to protection from enemy fire.

Common practices, US Army

Since an HMG platoon was often attached to a rifle company in the defense, that company's LMG section might be attached to one rifle platoon (often the reserve) and the HMG platoon's two sections to the other two platoons. The six MGs would work over the objective (especially villages) before the attack was launched. When in the defense, a tank or TD section attached to a rifle company might be placed under the weapons platoon leader, since his radio netted with the rifle company CO's set. In the attack, advancing rifle platoons would pause and wait for the MGs and mortars to set up to support the final assault. Once the planned artillery barrage was delivered, the 60mm and 81mm mortars and the cannon company would join in. Mortars would fire HE into trees to achieve air bursts over open positions; in the absence of trees, WP would be fired at open-topped positions to shower them with burning droplets. Assault troops learned how to maintain direction when attacking through lingering smoke.

Cannon and AT company platoons were often detailed to battalions and positioned as required by the battalion CO or even company COs, since this was more responsive to tactical requirements than trying to follow a regimental plan made before the current situation evolved. The regiment might retain control if a tank threat was expected from a particular direction. 60mm mortars were usually kept under company control; the battalion 81mm mortars might be under battalion control, or a section might be detailed to support each rifle company. There was no set methodology of attaching weapons to subunits. In another example, a company left one rifle platoon in its frontline position with both an LMG and an HMG section and one 60mm, while the rest of the company plus an HMG section was pulled back to prepare to meet an attack from a different direction.

As mentioned, underemployed battalion AT platoons and the regimental AT company often undertook secondary infantry duties, and the AT company's mine platoon might serve as a rifle platoon. In the absence of Panzers the AT guns still had their uses, however: direct fire support, securing

France, 1944: a crew load a US 60mm M2 mortar with an HE round (olive drab with yellow markings). In the attack the 60mm was sufficiently man-portable to follow the assault platoons, engaging identified and suspected enemy positions and laying smoke screens. For greater mobility the bipod and even the baseplate might be dispensed with, and the mortar would be fired hand-held with the base of the tube jammed into the ground or an earth-filled steel helmet, though this gave only marginal accuracy over a few hundred yards. (Tom Laemlein/Armor Plate Press)

The US 105mm M3 "snub-nosed" pack howitzer was fielded in 1943 as a more potent companion for the 75mm M1A1; six equipped the cannon company organic to infantry regiments, towed by 1½-ton cargo trucks. Weighing 955lb, it comprised a standard M2 howitzer barrel shortened to 66in, mounted on a modified 75mm pack howitzer carriage. It was capable of firing at 15rpm; maximum range was 8,295 yards with the 33lb HE round, and 3,000 yards with HEAT ammunition. The M3 used essentially the same ammunition as the 105mm M2A1 howitzer equipping divisional field artillery battalions, but with a lighter propellant charge to ensure complete combustion in the shorter barrel. This particular "shorty 105," of a glider artillery battalion of the US 82nd Abn Div, is being loaded into a Waco CG-4A. (Tom Laemlein/Armor Plate Press)

open flanks and gaps, and as a "fire brigade" to rush into emergency firing positions to increase fire in a given sector. Interestingly, 57mm gun crewmen sometimes removed the shield for better visibility and maneuverability when positioning guns by hand.

Cannon companies performed numerous roles: assault support and counterbattery fires, peripheral AT defense, and motorized reconnaissance, supply transport, and medical evacuation using the company's organic transport. When, as was often the case in US formations, there was abundant artillery, they might park their howitzers and reorganize as ad hoc infantry to help defend extended frontages. The company possessed three 29-man platoons each equipped with three 1½-ton trucks, a jeep, a bazooka, a .50cal machine gun, and three grenade launchers. The platoon's two squads or sections (based on the gun sections) might be filled out with extra personnel from the large platoon and company HQs, and the vehicles allowed the company to serve as a mobile reserve. It is possible that when serving as an ad hoc infantry company one or two 105mm howitzers might be retained for short-range defensive direct fire, but since cannon companies lacked BARs, LMGs, and mortars they were unsuited for offensive missions.

The US infantry battalion had six .50cal M2 machine guns: one per company weapons platoon, one each in the HQ company's ammunition and pioneer platoon and AT platoon, plus one in the heavy weapons company HQ. The regimental HQ company had two, the service company seven, and the cannon and AT companies three each. Within the regiment these 23 guns were mounted on truck cabs and lacked dedicated crews – gun crew was a secondary duty. Although mainly issued for AA use they were provided ground tripods, and some units formed provisional gun crews from HQ volunteers and battalion ammunition and pioneer platoons; however, only a small number of guns were employed in this manner, and for short periods.

EXAMPLE

US 2nd Armd Div vs German VGR 330, Geilenkirchen, October 1944

An example of both US and German practice is found in the defense of the *Westwall* in the vicinity of the Wurm and Ruhr rivers by the 183. Volksgrenadier-Division. This formation was raised in September 1944 from remnants of the 183. Infanterie-Division, virtually destroyed in the Brody Pocket in Byelorussia that July. Comprising surviving veterans, underemployed Luftwaffe and Kriegsmarine personnel, and Austrian conscripts, it was reinforced with the XVI Landwehr-Festungs-Bataillon, and Festungs-Maschinengewehr-Bataillon 42 ("Territorial Fortress" and "Fortress Machine-Gun" Battalions). These two units, manned by 40- to 50-year-olds, possessed four companies of World War I-vintage 7.92mm water-cooled MG08 HMGs. While obsolescent, these were feasible for positional defense owing to their heavy, stable mountings and accurate sustained-fire capability. At the beginning of October 1944 the division's Volksgrenadier-Regiment 330 was defending the Geilenkirchen area north of Aachen.

The US 2nd Armd Div was ordered to punch through the dragon's teeth and concrete bunkers of this sector of the "Siegfried Line." There was no continuous German frontline; defenses were centered on clusters of bunkers which were linked by an underground telephone system. The centralized command bunkers were further linked to artillery and mortar units in the rear, and could relay fire requests. German FOs were located well forward, observing the avenues of tank approach. It was understood that these bunker clusters could not be bypassed; they had to be totally defeated in order to prevent counterattacks, attacks from the rear, and the harassing of resupply elements, and furthermore they had to be destroyed to prevent them from being reoccupied.

The bunkers only allowed one or two MGs to be positioned inside, but others were dug in along with riflemen and *Panzerfaust* and *Panzerschreck* gunners in surrounding V- and L-shaped slit trenches covering all approaches. AT ditches were dug on ridge sides and in front of and to the flanks of many bunkers; AT mines were sometime sewn on AFV approaches, and some anti-personnel mines were laid. (Mines were later found stacked on roadsides where there had not been enough time to lay them, and some minefields were

An 8cm German mGrW34 mortar in a standard circular dug-in position in wintertime. The 3-rd steel ammunition cases also held fuzes and three propellant charges per round; ammo was additionally packed in 12-rd crates. A full seven-man crew man-packing the mortar carried 24 rounds. Each mortar "troop" was also supposed to have a one-horse, two-wheel If9 infantry cart to carry the mortar and ammunition, accompanied by a farrier. (Courtesy Concord Publications)

unguarded.) An occasional 7.5cm SP assault gun reinforced the position as a mobile pillbox, and these would prove more troublesome than the bunkers themselves. Making matters more difficult for the US infantry were the thick brush and saplings that had grown around the long-disused fortifications, providing excellent camouflage.

A' major surprise was that the many 8cm and 12cm mortars were positioned 3,000–4,000 yards behind the foremost bunkers. They were not placed far enough forward to range deep into American areas, but positioned to range on the bunkers' approaches and the bunkers themselves in order to barrage attackers. Some 7.5cm and 15cm infantry guns were also placed well to the rear. This made it extremely difficult to locate and counterbattery the mortars and guns. Moreover, once the Americans had defeated the bunkers they were in range of mortars and artillery too far ahead for the infantry to advance quickly and overrun them. They would first have to face counterattacks, and then consolidate before advancing further.

The terrain was hilly, densely forested, and wet with frequent rains that turned many areas, even on ridges and other high ground, into quagmires. Tanks were often restricted to asphalt and improved dirt roads. In some instances M5A1 Stuart light tanks could maneuver cross-country without

H SHOULDER-FIRED ANTITANK WEAPONS, 1943–45

Shoulder-fired rocket-propelled or recoilless weapons came into widespread use at company and platoon levels in 1943 and were fully accepted by 1944. They combined two comparatively old but recently much refined technologies: the shaped-charge warhead, and the compact high-velocity rocket. They allowed infantrymen to stalk and "kill" tanks with lightweight weapons by maneuvering into favorable firing positions; besides AT use, they also proved effective against field fortifications and buildings. They were issued in significant numbers, and proved to be a substantial threat to tank forces.

The Americans were the first to field such a weapon, with the 2.36in M1 AT rocket launcher ("bazooka" or "stovepipe") first used in November 1942 in North Africa; not illustrated here, it was identifiable by two forward handgrips. The improved and much more widely issued M1A1 (1) was fielded late in 1943. The M6, M6A1, and M6A2 HEAT rockets (1a) had a pointed nose and blade-type fins; early-production M6s were painted yellow with black markings. The M1A1 weighed 13lb 3oz, and was 54.5in long; at 250 yards' range it could penetrate 4in (100mm) of armor, and a crew could fire at 4–5rpm.

The greatly refined M9/M9A1 (2) appeared in 1944; this could be broken down into two barrel sections for ease of transport (3), the distinction being the improved barrel coupling on the M9A1. It weighed 15lb 4oz, and was 61in long; it could penetrate 5in (127mm) at 300 yards, and had a firing rate of 10rpm. The M6A3 HEAT round (2a), identifiable by its rounded head and drum-type enclosed fins, offered increased penetration, range, accuracy, and reliability. Some 2.36in smoke rockets were used late in the war for target-marking and blinding enemy positions. (See also Osprey Weapon 18, *The Bazooka*.)

The British "projector, infantry, antitank, Mk 1" or PIAT, pronounced "pee-at" (4), differed from tubular weapons in that the 3.5in Mk 1A HEAT bomb (4a) was placed in an open-top chute. Pulling the trigger released a powerful spring-loaded rod which kicked the bomb out and simultaneously ignited the propellant charge in its tailboom; in theory, this detonation also re-cocked the spring. (It was thus not strictly speaking a rocket launcher, and was far from being recoilless.) Before the first shot the PIAT spring had to be manually cocked, which required a prodigious physical effort. The projector weighed 32lb and was 39in long; its projectile could penetrate 4in (100mm) at its maximum range of 115 yards, and (if it re-cocked automatically) it had a rate of 4rpm.

Copying Lend-Lease bazookas captured from the Red Army, the Germans introduced the 8.8cm *Raketenpanzerbüchse 54* ("rocket [anti]armor weapon") on the Eastern Front in October 1943 (5). Weighing 24lb with the shield fitted and 20lb 11oz without, it was 65in long; it had a range of 200 yards, and a firing rate of 4–5rpm. Popularly called the *Panzerschreck* ("armor terror"), the RPzB54 was employed on all fronts; the very effective RPzBGr4322 rocket (5a) could penetrate 8in (200mm) of armor.

The *Panzerfauste* ("armor fists") were not rocket launchers, but a series of single-shot, one-man recoilless AT projectors held on top of the shoulder; a propellant charge in the tube expelled the over-caliber projectile. The first *Panzerfaust 30* (the number indicating its optimum range, in meters) appeared late in 1943 in two versions: the *klein* (small) had a 33mm tube and 95mm-diameter warhead, and the *groß* (large) a 44mm tube and 140mm warhead. The *Panzerfaust 60* and *100*, issued in mid- and late 1944, respectively, had the same tube length and warhead caliber as the *Panzerfaust 30 groß* but improved sights and firing systems; they were externally similar, but the *100* used two propellant charges. The *Panzerfaust 60* (6) was the most widely used model; it weighed 14lb 14oz, was 41.1in long, and could penetrate 6in (152 mm) of armor at 60 yards' range. The *Granate* projectile of the *60* and *100* is shown as (6a), removed from the launcher tube and thus with its spring-loaded fins unfolded. (See Osprey Weapon 36, *Panzerfaust and Panzerschreck*.)

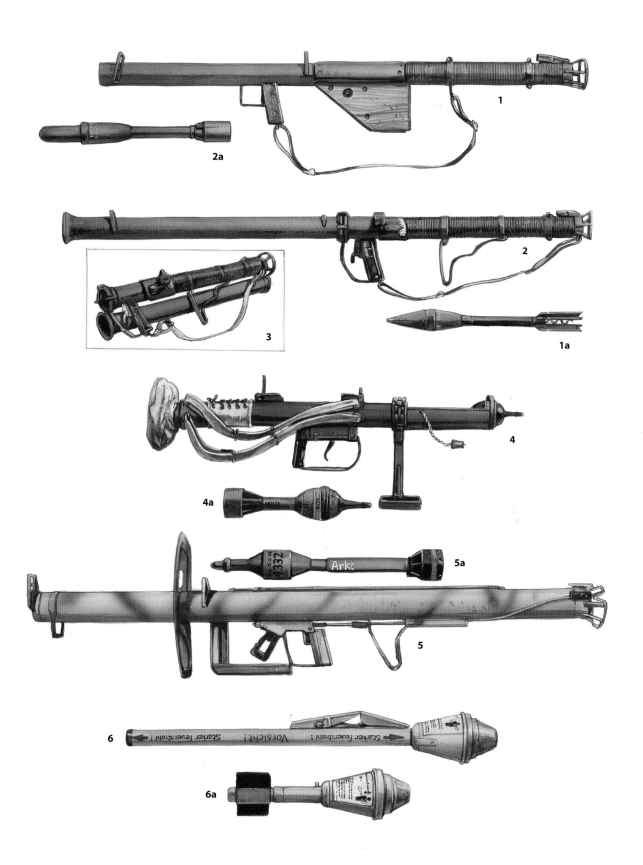

1

2a

1a

2

3

4

4a

5a

5

6

6a

Members of the Volkssturm home guard are sworn in, as desperate measures are taken to try to halt the Allied forces sweeping into Germany. They are armed with the *Panzerfaust 60,* but otherwise do not even seem to possess rifles or hand grenades. At right is an 8.8cm RPzB54 *Panzerschreck*; an alternative nickname was the same as that bestowed on the US bazooka from which it was copied – *Ofenrohr,* "stovepipe." (Tom Laemlein/Armor Plate Press)

bogging down, but the much heavier M4 Shermans frequently became mired. Roads often followed the tops and sides of ridges. Understanding that the terrain channeled the Americans onto the roads, the Germans focused on these rather than establishing broad linear defenses. As battalion task forces fought their way down the roads they would be confronted with numerous obstacles, and one ambush after another.

Volksgrenadier-Regiment 330, along with VGR 343 and 351 of 183. VG-Div, reorganized its fire support weapons, of which they lacked full allocations although they possessed some substitutes. The two battalions' heavy companies either lacked or had fewer than four 7.5cm infantry guns; these appear to have been placed under regimental control and concentrated deep in the rear under the regimental infantry-gun company. The battalion 8cm and regimental 12cm mortars (three and two platoons, respectively) were also concentrated in the rear, with platoons assigned specific roads that the Americans must advance along.

The Panzer-Zerstörer-Kompanie had two instead of three *Panzerschreck* platoons, plus three 7.5cm AT guns and two 5cm guns. The *Panzerschreck* platoons were divided between the different approach roads, but retained their structure of three two-man crews in each squad, and the crews were deployed roughly as specified in the *Panzerschreck* manuals. Each troop (squad) dug three positions, usually with two forward and one to the rear, no more than 150 meters apart laterally and front-to-rear; in this way the three crews could cover an area 450 meters deep and 300 meters wide. *Panzerschreck* positions consisted of a point-forward V-shaped trench with 2m- or 3m-long arms, allowing gunners to fire from either arm while the loader sheltered from the back blast in the other arm. They could fire in any direction; the three positions protected one another, and could take flanking and rear shots if tanks passed through the position. The V-shaped trenches were dug within brush-covered ground but close to the edge, to allow observation and clear shots; the soil was usually removed from the position, making them very difficult to identify even if in the open. In this engagement the VGR 330 teams tended to be deployed deeper in depth along the roads. Since these followed ridges they had steep slopes on at least one side; simply knocking the track off a road-bound tank effectively blocked the road, and allowed following halted tanks to be taken under fire. Tank retrievers were unable to come forward, so even repairable tanks had to be pushed off the road by following tanks. The five AT guns were positioned where they could take advantage of their range by firing down the long axis of roads. In these defilade positions the crews dug slit trenches between the spread gun trails to afford immediate cover from American mortar and tank fire.

Obstacles were emplaced at road chokepoints: sharp turns, sunken stretches, intersections, etc. These consisted of interlocking fallen trees (abatis), vertical posts, rubble from roadside buildings demolished with explosives, demolition craters, and small point minefields of AT and anti-personnel mines along with booby traps. A simple yet effective "roadblock" was a few crates, fence pickets, tree limbs, and boards tossed into a pile. A tank would have to halt while infantry came forward to check it for mines and booby traps, and once it halted *Panzerfaust* gunners, MGs, and sharpshooters would open fire.

When the 2nd Armd Div attacked up a one-lane asphalt road toward Geilenkirchen, this was covered by two concrete MG bunkers reinforced by dug-in infantry, three *Panzerschreck* squads, some Landwehr detachments armed with *Panzerfausts* and LMGs using ambush and hit-and-run tactics, a 7.5cm and a 5cm AT gun. Numerous German mortar concentrations were plotted on the road, the bunkers, and other positions.

One of the two light machine-gun squads of a rifle company's weapons platoon from US 65th Inf Div picking their way through Buss, Germany, in March 1945. The gunner (center) carries an M1919A6 Browning LMG with its bipod, metal shoulder stock, and carrying handle; the cone-shaped M8 flash-hider had not yet been fielded. The M1919A6 could also be fired from the M2 tripod like the M1919A4 that still armed most units. The supposedly improved M1919A6 was actually heavier than the M1919A4: the latter weighed 31lb without the tripod, and 45lb with it; the M1919A6 weighed 32lb 8oz without, and 46lb 6oz with it. Both were fed with 250-rd belts, and had a cyclic rate of 400–550rpm. (Tom Laemlein/Armor Plate Press)

As the first bunker was attacked by US tanks and infantry, suppressive HE and smoke mortar fire was placed on the second. This drove the outside defenders into the bunker, allowing additional American infantry to move in close. The first bunker was neutralized by tank fire through the embrasure and numerous satchel charges against the rear door, and the defenders surrendered. The mortar fire was lifted from the second bunker, and as the defenders rushed out to reoccupy their slit trenches the infantry cut many down with LMGs and BARs. The survivors, driven back inside, soon surrendered when tank and demolition attacks were launched.

The tank section advanced up the road hoping to position themselves on a flank to engage the expected counterattack, but the infantry tasked to accompany them were driven back by mortar fire and forced to shelter inside the captured bunkers with their prisoners. The lead tank was knocked out by the 7.5cm AT gun, blocking the road. The accompanying FO called for a "battery six" (24 rounds) of 155mm howitzer, and eliminated the AT gun. The remaining two tanks swung to the left and followed the ridge crest paralleling the road. After passing the burning tank on the road they were ambushed at close range by three dug-in *Panzerschreck* crews. One tank was hit three times and de-tracked; the other was hit once, and launched 2in smoke rounds to cover its withdrawal. The infantry LMGs and BARs opened fire, but the 60mm mortars could not find a clear position to fire from; 81mm fire was called for, and the rounds air-burst in the trees over the three *Panzerschreck* positions. The remaining tank commander refused to advance alone. German LMG and sniper fire was coming from further down the ridge; the FO called for another "battery six" of 155mm, and a 105mm battery also contributed fire. (This was a common practice; untasked artillery units monitored radios and added their fire to other units' missions.)

The crew of a US 57mm M1 antitank gun manhandle the weapon down an alley to a new firing position in a German town, 1945. AT guns proved effective in urban fighting, being able to penetrate medium-weight masonry and place shots through windows, doors, and firing ports. The 57mm M1 was an improved copy of the British 6-pdr Mk II; comparative figures with the 6-pdr Mk IV were a weight of 2,810lb (6-pdr, 2,471lb) and barrel length of 117in (6-pdr, 94.2in). The ammunition was interchangeable, however, and the performance identical; the 6lb 4oz AP round penetrated 2.7in (68mm) of armor at 1,000 yards, and the rate of fire was 12–14rpm. It was of limited value against Panthers and Tigers, but in fact most Panzers encountered in 1944–45 were lighter PzKw IVs.

The 57mm M1 began replacing the impotent 37mm M3A1 in mid-1943, at a ratio of three 57mm guns for every four 37mm. The prime mover was a 1½-ton 6 x 6 cargo truck carrying the 10-man crew, ammunition, and gun equipment. Each crew was additionally armed with a 2.36in bazooka. With nine 57mm guns in the regimental AT company and three in each of the infantry battalion HQ companies, totaling 18 guns, plus 157 bazookas, the US infantry regiment was generously provided with AT weapons. (Tom Laemlein/ Armor Plate Press)

After the artillery pasting the US infantry advanced along the ridge crest and road, finding numerous German dead and taking a few stunned prisoners. A destroyed 5cm AT gun was discovered; it had covered a heavy log roadblock, which was mined and booby-trapped. Engineers were called forward to blow the roadblock, but more small-arms and MG fire snapped overhead. Expecting a counterattack, the infantry took up hasty positions; a couple of halfhearted German probes were delivered, but a serious counterattack never developed. Several 8cm and 12cm mortar barrages struck throughout the area, probably accompanied by infantry-gun fire. With the light fading, the infantry advanced another 100 yards and dug in for the night. An HMG platoon reinforced the company, and a suitable position was found for the 60mm mortars. Through the night there were sporadic enemy probes and mortar and infantry-gun fire. Patrols dispatched at first light found that the Germans had withdrawn; reinforced with tanks, the advance continued.

The Germans had made good use of limited resources, organizing their defenses on the bunkers which served mainly as shelters. They had incorporated the terrain well, reinforcing the channeled road and steep, muddy slopes with obstacles and mines. Weak in infantry, they used MGs to good effect. The close-range *Panzerschreck* and *Panzerfaust* ambushes were also effective; the Germans made very good use of their mortars and infantry guns, positioning them too far back for the US infantry to overrun. Their major weaknesses were their lack of sufficient artillery, which could have been devastating to infantry, and of mobile reserves reinforced by armor to conduct meaningful counterattacks.

The Netherlands, 1944: a mortar squad of the 48th Armd Inf Bn, US 7th Armd Div, fire an 81mm M1 mortar from a halftrack M21 mortar carrier. It could be dismounted for ground firing, and in that configuration it weighed 136lb. With a 49.5in barrel, its minimum and maximum ranges were 100 and 3,290 yards, and the light and heavy 81mm HE rounds weighed 6lb 14oz and 10lb 10oz, respectively.
There were four mortar carriers in an armored infantry battalion's mortar platoon, part of the HQ company. The earlier M4 carrier had the mortar facing rearward, which proved to be tactically undesirable. The halftrack had stowage for 97 mortar rounds, and both the M4 and M21 had a crew of six. Note the M1A1 AT mines in the external rack; these were laid around night defensive positions, frequently without burying them, and were recovered before moving out. (Tom Laemlein/Armor Plate Press)

CONCLUSION

There is little doubt that the various fire support weapons, offering a wide range of capabilities, played a key tactical role on World War II battlefields. This included direct and indirect fires capable of destroying or neutralizing all manner of targets: personnel, AFVs, support vehicles, field fortifications, defended buildings, obstacles, and more. Their role was often understated, overlooked, and taken for granted. They were not always necessary, nor employed to their maximum capabilities; but it was better to have an abundance of specialized fire support units than to discover a need for them when embroiled in combat. Fire support platoons and companies habitually operated broken up with their elements supporting line companies. Even on occasions when all or part of the available fire support units (for example, regimental cannon companies) were not needed owing to an abundance of field artillery available to a division, the infantry might well be glad of them again soon afterwards.

The gradual postwar transformation of armies saw the retention of some types of fire support weapons, often in modified forms, while others were discarded or replaced with new weapons systems, but it was not until the early 1960s that this evolution was essentially completed. Machine-gun units, other than platoons at battalion level, quickly disappeared; water-cooled HMGs were soon relegated to history books, and the lighter, more portable general-purpose machine guns usable in both light (bipod) and heavy (tripod) roles became standard. The long-range, indirect-fire role of machine guns all but disappeared as more accurate and responsive mortars and artillery made this role virtually unnecessary.

Mortars remained, with essentially the same role: immediate fire support at company and battalion levels. They now tend to be employed in centralized sections or platoons rather than being attached in ones and twos in direct support to infantry subunits. Operating more like artillery, with centralized fire control and assigned FOs, mortars also have a wider variety of projectiles and fuzing to expand their utility. With the advent of low-intensity conflicts and an abundance of artillery, mortars somewhat fell from use, but they have remained important assets.

Antitank guns were quickly phased out after World War II, being replaced by man-portable, shoulder-fired rocket launchers as well as light vehicle-transported recoilless rifles. The former continued to evolve into ever more lethal weapons, and remain in use today. Recoilless rifles, with improved HEAT and new specialized projectiles, developed into useful AT weapons that were also able to fulfill many supporting direct-fire roles, but in the 1970s they themselves were mostly replaced with AT wire-guided missiles. While the burdensome and only marginally effective AT rifles had almost disappeared by 1945, a derivative family has evolved since the 1980s as large-caliber, telescope-sighted anti-personnel and anti-materiel rifles. Infantry guns quickly disappeared after the war, made redundant by light artillery, improved mortars, recoilless rifles, and to a lesser extent by 30mm and 40mm automatic grenade launchers.

SELECT BIBLIOGRAPHY

Chappell, Mike, *The Vickers Machine Gun* (The British Soldier in the 20th Century No. 8) (Okehampton, Devon; Wessex Military Publishing, 1989)

Copp, Terry, *The Brigade: The Fifth Canadian Infantry Brigade in World War II* (Mechanicsburg, PA; Stackpole Books, 1992)

Courtney, Richard D., *Normandy to the Bulge: An American Infantry GI in Europe During World War II* (Carbondale, PA; Southern Illinois University Press, 1997 – regimental AT company)

Forty, George, *British Army Handbook 1939–1945* (Phoenix Mill, UK; Sutton Publishing, 1998)

Lubbeck, William, with David Hurt, *At Leningrad's Gate: The Story of a Soldier with Army Group North* (Havertown, PA; Casemate, 2010 – regimental infantry-gun company)

Macdonald, Charles B., *Company Commander: The Classic Infantry Memoir of World War II* (Ithaca, NY; Buford Books, 1999)

Mansoor, Peter R., *The GI Offensive in Europe: The Triumph of American Infantry Divisions, 1941–1945* (Lawrence, KS; University Press of Kansas, 1999)

Zaloga, Steven J. and Leland S. Ness, *Red Army Handbook 1939–45* (Phoenix Mill, UK; Sutton Publishing, 2003)

US Army, *Breaching the Siegfried Line: XIX Corps 2 to 16 October 1944* (West Chester, OH; The Nafziger Collection, 2015) http://www.nafzigercollection.com/

US Army, *Handbook on the British Army with Supplement*, TM 30-410 (13 September 1942)

US Army, *Handbook on U.S.S.R. Military Forces*, TM 30-430 (1 March 1946)

US Army, *Handbook on German Military Forces*, TM-E 30-451 (1 March 1945)

INDEX

Note: page numbers in bold refer to illustrations, captions and plates.

Figures in **bold** refer to illustrations.